Smokey

by

Theodore Grant

riverrun press

Smokey

ISBN 978-0-9540024-3-5

Published by Riverrun Press

www.riverrunpress.co.uk

First published in Great Britain 1993

This edition 2010

Smokey is a true story.

When a couple decided to emigrate to Canada, they gave their pet cat to Theodore and Josie. A common enough occurrence one would think, but was it? Smokey decided he was very much one of the family.

To cat lovers everywhere

I

It has never been easy for the run-of-the-mill man or woman to purchase a house, and it does not get any easier. Nor has it ever been - and one may hope it never will be - impossible.

'Thirteen wasted years' screamed a newspaper headline, heralding the advent of Harold Wilson as Prime Minister. Looking back, I am sure that the person who coined that slogan, and most other people, whatever their political persuasion, would now agree that those years were not so bad after all.

How black it all seemed in 1958. It was the full stop of the Stop-Go era. House prices on the up and up, mortgages at a record 7% and difficult to obtain, trouble in Europe, likewise in the rest of the world.

We - my wife Josie and I - had been saving long and hard to accumulate the necessary deposit and if for every two steps forward we slipped back one, still it was progress of a sort. Nor did we consider the inconveniences of major importance. The objective was clear and an inspiration in itself. A home of our own.

The cheapest meals in the cheapest cafés, the rationing of cigarettes to ourselves of twenty per week, the going without of many of the things considered by our contemporaries as essentials.

We lived in a furnished room, not a flat, but a large bed-sitter that looked out onto a humdrum street. It lacked the taken-for-granted amenities of modern life such as television, refrigerator, washing machine and spin dryer. We did not possess a car, putting this in a much lower order of priority than was the norm.

Some luxuries we did permit ourselves, for when all is said and done life has to be lived, and time spent in an endless grind proves the truth of the adage about Jack, work and play.

An occasional visit to the cinema or theatre was not opulence, a dance now and then was cheap and enjoyable. Exhibitions, art galleries and the like titillated the senses at no cost at all. Add to this the one extravagance of an annual holiday, which we told ourselves we needed, and it appeared to us that by adopting moderation in everything we were being eminently purposeful toward our objective - our future house.

In the jargon of the London landladies we were Business People. That is we left the apartment each morning - Monday to Friday - travelled to the West End to perform mundane jobs in offices, and returned to our nest, i.e. furnished room, every evening. Like so many nine to five workers, such was our existence; strap hangers of the tube united, but microcosms of the teeming patch that is the capital.

It was a joint venture and that was the full fun, enjoyment, satisfaction and exhilaration of it. We had been separate entities, that is alone, leading, we hoped, reasonably worthwhile lives, but on the whole, aimless. We had met and joined forces in the great endeavour called marriage and after the settling-in period, planned for the future together. A house of our own was not to be a pipe-dream of youth never to materialise, despite what some said, or a burden round our necks as said others. To people who had had life easy it was a modest enough ambition, but let them talk to countless numbers of people who struggle on year after year in rented accommodation!

Whilst saving like Midas and his queen, we were also paradoxically spending, carefully of course and with the one object, or was it mirage, in view.

Each Saturday morning we left the bed-sit about ten, and journeyed to a London suburb to look at and sum up the district, for we reasoned that the locality was an important aspect of the plan. It had to be nice, not too conventional and within comfortable commuting distance of the centre of the metropolis. Nevertheless, far enough away from the hustle, dirt and noise of Victoria and the West End. A whole list of names comes to mind for I think we visited Dagenham, Streatham, Harrow, Finchley and all other areas between. We still have one of the finest collections of local maps outside of the libraries.

Suburbs bad, good and indifferent were scanned with a hopeful or jaundiced eye. Hampstead was turned down on the grounds that it was too close, too plush and far too expensive which was a pity for we really liked the area. It was a difficult decision and we went there twice, taking the opportunity each time to visit the quaint little cinema that showed such unusual and antique films.

Eventually as our cash accumulated we narrowed our choice and short-listed three places that we felt were nearest to our requirements. They were - not in order of precedence - Bromley, Wembley and Wimbledon. Each possessed attributes that we considered to our taste and above average.

We obtained the names and addresses of the district estate agents from local newspapers and wrote to them. Soon brochures and property details were arriving by every post, a bewildering assortment of duplicated print that threatened to clog. We made up our minds that if and when we finally achieved our goal we would make it our first task to paper a room completely with a mosaic of the sheets.

Many places were outside our price range, some were too large and, surprisingly, some were too small. All considered it was part of the joy of house-hunting, which is probably why the main word in our vocabulary those days was 'frustration.' There was an excellent house at Wembley - so said the brochure - with all mod. cons. How that description was put together I shall never know, for although from the outside the house looked resplendent with enough fresh paint in evidence to warrant us requesting a key, once we were inside the house we were horrified. There were damp patches on the walls, holes in the wainscot, and there was every indication that the amount of renovation that would be needed would cost many hundreds of pounds. A wasted trip that was to be the first of many.

After several months we came across a house at Bromley that fulfilled our expectations and we were very excited as we went ahead with a purchase. For the first time, we discovered a whole new language of legal jargon. Such phrases as 'all that messuage', 'local land charges' and 'subject to contract' were read with wonderment and we blissfully anticipated the final 'completion date'. After a few weeks the whole thing fell through merely because the owner changed his mind. In due course we received a bill from our solicitors for 'abortive purchase'. We were despondent and that was not the only setback.

We were beaten to the post for a dwelling at Wimbledon, although we considered it a blessing in disguise as Josie thought the raised, stainless-steel, solid fuel fireplace a bit too grand and dominating to live with. A marvellous prospect in the same district was rather beyond our means, and whilst the estate agent went to great pains to arrange a second mortgage, he failed and so we said goodbye to that also.

Had we, we wondered, been altogether too choosy, or was it that the fates decreed that we should go on living in our Victoria bed-sit? The conversation ebbed and flowed till one evening Josie remarked, "There's one district in our travels we've rather overlooked."

"Where, for heaven's sake, is that?"

"Richmond."

"Altogether too far out. It's miles away in Surrey."

"One of the girls at work comes in from there."

"Maybe. Some folk commute from Brighton, and even further, but I don't fancy that. The fares would cost a bomb and we would have to leave so early in the morning that we'd be half asleep all day. Also, and this I know, it's a very pricey area, and you would have to be at least an executive to buy a house there."

"It was just a thought."

Josie looked disappointed at my cool reception of her idea.

To settle the matter, we looked it up on a map and I was surprised to find that it was much closer to London than I had thought. Certainly nearer than Bromley and some of the other places we had visited. Furthermore it was on the tube network, and additional investigation revealed that it had very good rail connections. The time-table stated that the normal fast train time from Richmond to Waterloo was fourteen minutes. We hoped this was not a misprint.

Following my usual routine, I made a reconnaissance on the next Saturday. In this instance I got off the tube at Kew Gardens and, armed with my notebook, made various jottings: actual time of journey, names and addresses of estate agents obtained from their advertising boards and the general amenities of the area. I walked right along Sandycombe Road, branched right along Lower Mortlake Road, into Richmond town, and back along the Kew Road, returning to The Quadrant and out again to Ham. After a quick lunch I scoured the area, east to Sheen and west to Twickenham. The more I saw of the place, the more I liked it, and that despite the growing fatigue of the exercise.

Meanwhile, Josie, who had gone to Wimbledon to view another prospect - not a good one as it turned out - sat patiently in a café where, to justify her presence there, she had spent over two hours, drinking tea, and wondering if I had had an accident.

"Well?"

I endeavoured to hold back the enthusiasm I felt for we had known those other disappointments.

"It's got possibilities."

"Did you get the local paper?"

"Yes."

"Street Guide?"

"Yes."

"Agents' addresses?"

"Of course."

"Any suitable houses?"

"There might be."

"Stop trying to hide your smile, Theodore, and come right out with the prospects."

"On the face of it I must confess they're good but don't get all carried away by it. It's a nice town and the river has boats on it and there's a theatre. What they're charging for the houses, God only knows."

My words unheeded, Josie gave a cry of delight. "Great!"

It was ten o'clock before we got back to Victoria, but after a quick meal we wrote off for details of any suitable properties and by the following Thursday had received the replies. There were three properties on the current market, all within our price range and all within walking distance of the railway station. On paper, at least, all highly desirable.

"At last we seem to be getting somewhere," Josie said.

"Never count your chickens before they're hatched."

"Oh, I do hope they will hatch this time."

Bright and early on the Saturday morning I was back in Richmond, accompanied now by Josie. She wore a smart anorak which rather showed up my old grey raincoat which I fondly called my slouch-mac. It was drizzling.

The first two houses we called at were occupied and in each case, after a perusal of the outside, we knocked and asked if we could look over the interior. The occupants were only too pleased to oblige and our excitement was growing for they both looked very reasonable. The second one was smart and cosy although a more than average amount of furniture raised a brief suspicion in my mind that the items could be deliberately placed so as to hide defects. Naturally we said we would let them know.

The third house also appeared to have a lot to recommend it, bearing in mind the very reasonable price, but it was empty as was its neighbour. Why was this, I wondered? Two largish houses, newly painted, very cheap, side by side and both crying out to be occupied. Josie had no such doubts. "This is it!"

"Hold on. Remember the chickens. It's probably falling down inwards and even if not, there's a whole ramification of snags ahead, I expect. Anyway, we'd better get the keys from the agent."

We then noticed that the property we were interested in had two agents' boards outside. I knew this meant in all probability that the house had been on the market for some considerable time. Couldn't they get rid of it and if not, why?

I grunted in reply to Josie's enthusiastic comment that she felt it in her bones that this was *the* house. My natural caution had been sharpened by previous disappointments, but I had to admit that to the untrained eye it was a fine-looking Georgian edifice.

A rather extraordinary event took place before the morning was through which deepened my vague uneasiness. The gentleman in the estate agent's office would have nothing to do with us. From our, by now, considerable experience of house-hunting, we knew full well that in the normal run of things, agents were usually more than pleased to show prospective buyers round their properties, often too eager to hand over the keys and point out the advantages of the place.

We were on our guard against blandishments and found the chilly reception we now received puzzling, odd and, for us, embarrassing.

Perhaps he thought we were wasting his time, and he had no need to accompany us to the house if there was something on the radio he wanted to listen to. My slouch-mac may have given him the impression that we had not a penny to our name in which case he was not a very good judge of people and a very poor agent. He looked us up and down as if we were impecunious insects, answered our questions evasively and flatly refused to come with us or give us access. We left his office bewildered and crestfallen.

"So much for your bones, Josie," I said as we meandered towards the station.

"Wait a minute. What about the other agent?"

"Might as well look them up but we didn't make a note of their address."

We walked back to the house and from there to the other agents who fortunately weren't very far away. We were lucky, too, for it was five minutes to one o'clock, at which time they closed. In answer to my nervous enquiry the fellow looked up from his desk and smiled.

"Oh yes, I know the place. An excellent proposition, sir. You'll have to take the keys as I'm going off duty shortly but you'll find everything in order. Please make sure that you lock all the doors before you leave and drop the keys in our letter box."

He made a note of our names and address, wished us well and said he hoped to hear from us again. A few minutes later we turned the key in the front door and entered.

What we saw was a hallway which looked as if it had been recently decorated although there was no smell of paint. The wallpaper was a pink yellow flowery pattern and at the end of the passage was a glass door leading to the back garden. We explored the rooms and found them all newly decorated. The windows were extremely dirty and I again had a few misgivings for it seemed to indicate a long period of emptiness and this was confirmed by the garden which was overgrown with many and varied weeds. However, in such circumstances, one is inclined to overlook minor blemishes. Already I was mentally up on a ladder with a bucket of water and cloth, and a few hours on the garden would soon put it to rights.

We spent nearly an hour there and as we stood before the closed front door ready to leave, Josie spread her arms in the air.

"My bones never lie to me. They tell me that we've struck oil here. We will be as snug as bugs in rugs. You, me and the cat."

"Cat? What cat?"

"We must have one. No home is complete without a little pussy-cat."

Somewhat bemused by the day's events, I thrust aside lingering negative doubts.

"Agreed. It'll be just you, me and the mog."

II

I reminded my wife on the way back to the estate agent of the saying that there was many a slip 'twixt cup and lip. She was convinced that we had at last found the place we were looking for, but I insisted that we should think about it for a couple of days before proceeding further.

"If we think about it for too long it will go. Someone else will snap it up and we will once again be back to square one."

This I well knew could be the case and it was just the two days before we wrote. We had made up our minds and commenced the formalities of making an offer close enough to the asking figure to be considered, and received a counter-proposal.

The routine deposit on the purchase price of a property was ten per cent and not wishing to be burdened with a high mortgage, we made ours twenty per cent, naturally, of course, 'subject to contract'. This would place us under considerable initial strain but fortunately we were both, as far as we knew, healthy, and were working, and the going should therefore become easier.

So the rigmarole of legal technicalities wound its weary way forward and whenever the subject came up, as it often did, we merely crossed our fingers and hoped for the best. Despite our outlay, which we were assured was above the average, there were difficulties. The first major snag was that we were not considered riskworthy by any of the major building societies. To quote another piece of jargon, as the wife's income does not count when it comes to assessment and as you have no further collateral the project cannot proceed'. This meant that as we did not already own a house, did not possess any bonds or the like, and had no guarantors, we would be unable to keep up the repayments.

One after another the replies to our letters arrived all stating with a variety of phrases that they were unable to help. The agent was getting anxious as the seller wanted to close the deal.

One morning I received a phone call at work from the same gentleman who had given us the keys and who subsequently had been handling our case.

"Mr. Grant," said the voice, "can you go this lunch hour to The Scotch Hoose in Charing Cross Road?"

"I suppose so, but what's it for?"

"You may very well find it worth your while. Get there at one. You will see a gentleman there about five feet nine, dressed in grey or navy blue and with a rose in his buttonhole. His name is Mr. Chudwallah. Introduce yourself. Buy him a drink and a sandwich. Have a chat."

"Right. Mr. Chudwallah. The Scotch Hoose, one p.m. What's it all mean?"

"Rose in buttonhole. Let me know how you get on. Goodbye."

To say it put me in a fix is an understatement. I felt I was James Bond, acting on the instructions of M and about to meet Goldfinger. Unlike Bond, I was far from cool.

I duly arrived at the pub and kept my appointment with Mr. Chudwallah, who was a middle-aged English gentleman, slightly balding and, somewhat as I expected, wore dark glasses. Mr. Chudwallah had already had a few drinks, the slurring of his voice was unmistakable but I bought him another and a sandwich, and we talked.

We chatted about the weather, about films - and about gardening, at which Eric Chudwallah was an expert and I a primitive amateur. I bought him another drink and told him I had to get back to work by two. He nodded and we shook hands. I understood his closing remarks very clearly although he was very much under the influence.

"Don't worry about anything. The loan will be arranged. It will be eight per cent over fifteen years, you to pay all costs."

I had already told Josie of my assignment and she could hardly wait till I was in the room.

"First the bad news."

"Come on. Come on. What is it?"

"Eight per cent over fifteen years plus costs. Can we afford it?"

"Yes, we can and we must. What's the good news?"

"That's it. It's there if we want it. The house at Richmond that you've fallen in love with. All you have to do is say 'yes' and all I have to do is sign on the dotted line."

Despite our hefty deposit and our final attainment of the loan, snags remained. We worked it out that we were still four hundred pounds short of the agreed price and there would be legal fees to be paid. Fortunately the estate agent said there would be no trouble arranging a second mortgage and when we told our solicitor of the position, he was very understanding, telling us we could have two months' grace.

We turned down the idea of having the house surveyed in the confident knowledge that we had been all over the house ourselves and found it in good order. Had we not examined it in every detail? By now my suspicions had completely vanished and I was looking forward to the great day as much as Josie.

We had no furniture, which meant there would be no

moving costs. On the other hand we had little spare money to buy any, but we did not worry about this as we were prepared to start with the absolute minimum. So unashamedly short were we that when the agent rang us up to say that no further snags were expected and therefore we could, if we so wished, go round and put up curtains, we laughed for we knew that we could not afford to do it. We decided to sleep at the back of the house and not to worry about neighbours complaining, for if they did we could put up a blanket as a temporary measure. We drew the line at sleeping on the floor and decided to buy, on hire purchase, two fold-up beds to get over the first few nights. We arranged for them to be delivered on the day we moved.

"God help us if they don't arrive," I said. "I don't exactly fancy sleeping rough on a cold night."

Even Josie's smile faded at that grim thought.

We both went to the solicitor's office for the final signing ceremony with completion date settled for February fourteenth, which Josie considered a good omen.

All our possessions were in a couple of suitcases, one holdall and an assortment of carrier bags. On the evening before the day, we loaded up the carriers with miscellaneous articles of little value, travelled down to Richmond and left them in the porch. Both advertising boards were still on display but instead of the 'For Sale' signs, there were notices that said 'Sold'.

We had taken it for granted that the weather would be fine and so it was, but very cold. The following morning we made our last visit to the agents to get the keys and in less than ten minutes we were inside the 'well-appointed, much desired residence.'

The feeling of at last owning a home of our own was almost overpowering and I am sure that if the beds had been there we would have collapsed on them. As it was, we embraced, then went outside to take our photographs standing by the 'Sold' signs. Now it was a question of waiting for the gasman, the electrician and the delivery man.

I found the main stop-cock for the water and went up to the bathroom to test. There came an anguished yell from my wife. "Turn if off! Turn it off! You're flooding the house!"

Running downstairs I surveyed the scene. Water was pouring through the ceiling. It was not a good start.

"We should have checked this," I said.

"Yes. *We* should!"

"Go out and find a plumber and tell him it's absolutely top priority. I'll hang on and see if the beds arrive."

Whilst Josie was gone, I found some rags and mopped up as best I could. The gasman arrived. After examining the meter he shook his head.

"Sorry mate. I can't do anything. The pipes are blocked off and I'll have to send another man round. You can show him where you want your fire and cooker and get him to give you an estimate."

"When will he call?"

"Well it won't be today, that's for sure."

I thanked him and contented myself with the thought that as we did not have any appliances to fix, the matter was not urgent.

Next came the man from the Electricity Board and we were a little more fortunate. We could have the lights on immediately. However, the man explained that the meter and fuse box were not geared for power points and a new meter would have to be fitted. If we wanted points we would then have to get an estimate for the work to be done.

After he had departed, I was philosophising that as we were complete amateurs, we must expect to make all kinds of silly mistakes, when Josie returned.

She had been fortunate to find a plumber who had promised to call round before the day was out.

"Let's sit down calmly and think it out," I said.

"Sit down where?"

"Good grief! The beds aren't here yet and we haven't a chair between us. Be a good girl again, will you go and find a greengrocer who'll let you have a couple of orange boxes, and while you're about it see if you can get some logs. If the coalman doesn't call we're liable to freeze to death tonight."

Josie was gone a long time and although I still had an overcoat on, I was shivering. When she returned, she had obtained the orange boxes and also two straight-backed chairs that she had purchased from a second-hand furnishers. Just as we sat down the beds arrived. We placed them in the back room and considered it a good time to at last go to lunch. We left the front door open and pinned a note for the plumber on it.

After the meal we went round the shops. With only a little spare cash we were careful with our purchases, concentrating on the essentials. We bought sheets, blankets and pillows from one place and a quantity of logs from another, before returning to our home.

With the aid of crumpled-up newspapers, we got a fire going in an old-fashioned grate in our prospective sleeping quarters and it was nice to see the flames flying up the chimney.

There were still things to be done, some of them urgent,

and this time I left Josie to await the plumber, as I went back to the shops. Our staple provisions were to be bread, milk, tea, sugar, sausages and beans, with some utensils including kettle, teapot, mugs, frying pan, saucepan and cutlery. I also ordered milk and newspapers to be delivered and hoped that whoever came along with them, would not think that a mistake had been made and that it was the same old empty house. We knew it was not.

When I returned the man was already at work in the bathroom. He informed us that the trouble was due to a burst pipe underneath the bath probably caused by a freeze-up earlier in the winter. I expected him to ask for payment on the spot, which would have been fair enough but hard luck on him, as our funds would have been too low to meet his requirements. I heaved a sigh of relief when he said he would send his bill in to us. We thanked him profusely and he said he appreciated our comments and would do any other work we might require.

When he had gone I looked around the almost bare room and sighed with relief and contentment. Despite the sparsity it was beginning to look something like a home.

I placed sheets of newspaper on one of the orange boxes which would serve as a table and took it over to where the beds stood - in the corner of the room away from the window. The chairs were placed before the fire. We were sorry that the coal had not arrived, but the logs were cheerful enough. Whilst Josie made up the beds I judiciously placed some of our personal and beloved knick-knacks around the room. At one end of the shelf a tiny plastic statuette of a girl holding the world in her hands and her twin sister facing her at the other; in the middle, our favourite china ornament - a little ballerina we called Manina. I was just thinking the thought when Josie uttered it.

"East, West - home's best."

We cooked our first meal in the frying-pan over the blazing log fire, sausages and beans helped down with bread and cups of tea. It tasted good.

An exciting hour was spent sorting out our meagre belongings. Books were placed on a shelf that ran along a wall sideways to the window, clothes unpacked from the suitcases and arranged in carrier bags on the floor, and our small mains radio fitted up with a plug suitable for the only available socket. Indeed this was the only point in the whole of the house and would certainly not overload the few amps the present meter would carry.

There was a butler sink in the little room that led off from the one we were living in, which had probably been a scullery in the days when the house had more exalted occupants. Beyond this small room on the garden side was a small window with frosted glass and iron bars across it. For what purpose it had been designed we could only guess, but it led directly into a small raised part of the garden under which we knew was a shed. There was only one cupboard in our room, large enough to have been a pantry and the solid looking beam near the top looked as if it could have had flitches of bacon hanging from it at some time in the distant past.

I looked from the bare floorboards to the plain white ceiling and downwards at the hanging light bulb, which as yet was unshaded. It cast a garish yellow light completely in keeping with the rest of the scene. We had always intended to start with next to nothing and as things had turned out we had had to, but hopefully we could work upwards to better things. I felt sure we were both contented and that at least was a good thing.

We put a few more logs on the fire, undressed and each got into bed. The radio gave us news of the outside world that could have been from another planet so little was its impact. Dreamy music followed. It was past midnight.

"Do you think Manina is happy?" I enquired, repeating a little game we carried on from time to time.

"I'm sure she is and I can tell you she's awfully tired, too."

"Goodnight, then."

"Goodnight."

It was difficult to slumber. The eternal background noise of Victoria and the West End was missing and in its place the comparative quiet of Richmond was a deathly hush.

It would take quite a few nights to acclimatise from that bedsitter just a few miles away to this suburban outpost. The following morning would be Saturday, so we would be in no rush to arise. Our great day was over. At last I fell asleep.

It seemed only a matter of minutes before I awoke. There was a sound coming from outside that I had never heard before - the singing in unison of many birds. It was the dawn chorus which I had read about but never experienced and its effect surpassed that of any alarm clock. It went on for several minutes then quickly faded.

We got up in time to receive the coalman at ten o'clock and we were glad to have the five hundredweights of solid fuel, for the logs, although useful, were only a stop-gap. Also the house, neglected as it had been for some time, needed to be rid of the cold and damp.

We spent a quiet weekend, wrote a few letters, listened to the radio and in the evening rang up Josie's parents to tell them how we had got on. In short, we settled in.

Monday morning saw us chasing along the road to Richmond Station, to catch the 8.13 to Waterloo.

That evening, Josie told me about a colleague who worked in the same building as herself and whom she saw occasionally.

Nora and her husband Bert were fed up with the state of the country and had been trying for some time to emigrate to Canada. After many months they had been given the date on which their ship would be sailing. They would be leaving at the end of the month, and had various items of furniture to dispose of in a hurry.

They were also looking for a good home for their cat.

As we were both enthusiastic about the idea of a nice feline pet to complete our ménage, we welcomed the chance of receiving 'Smokey'.

Popular belief states that the world's population can be divided into two camps, one lot loving cats and the other hating them. Contrary to this, I believed there was a third force - a sizeable minority who liked cats as pets, but did not dote on them. I believed that my wife and I were of that third section of humanity. Both of us came from cat-orientated families and could look back on a succession of pets that our parents had befriended.

It was nice to have one about the house, to play with it and see that it was well looked after, and it was sad to see it go, especially if one did not know the going - but it was soon replaced.

Only once during my childhood did we have a dog as a pet and for some reason or other he was given away after a few weeks. That is not to say that my parents disliked dogs and nor did I, but we never had the true accord with them that one should. The cat, on the other hand, was an independent creature, clean in its habits, and did not have to be unduly worried about. Also, it did not cost much to keep, an important consideration in our home where it had to eat what was put down for it or, as my mother used to say, "do the other thing."

Josie's parents belonged to the clan of positive devotees. There was hardly a stray that found its way to their home that was refused admittance. They actively encouraged any cast-off feline to cross the doorstep and stay. Her father, in particular, worshipped the ground their little paws walked on; thus, when one of his small furry friends passed on there was gloom in the house for weeks. He was definitely maudlin even when the subject came up long after the event.

There was one cat out of the many that he had particularly adored, a queen called Fifi. The cat, after a long and happy life, had died of old age and been buried at the bottom of the garden with all the rites due to its kind. The tiny grave was furnished with a headstone, inscription and cross. He was fond of recalling the incident with sadness in his eyes, relishing every last nuance of sentimental remembrance. It was said that his Gallic ancestry was responsible for this extreme sensitivity, although I have never regarded the French as a particularly soft-hearted nation, songs notwithstanding.

At one time, if my wife is to be believed, and I think she is, there were nine cats in the household. Fortunately it was a large house. Each cat was a different variety and each, for various odd reasons, was given a name. Apart from Fifi, who I had met when she was on her last legs, I had made the acquaintance of Bunny, Chubby and George. They had got on well with one another, and there was never, as one would have expected, a smell in the house.

The most cats we had had in our family had been two at one time.

That parents hand on their traits, in part at least, to their children is self-evident. Although Josie did not have her father's almost pathological love of cats, there was something of it there.

As a child she had heard that the neighbours' cat was to be put down as they were leaving the district. For once in a way it was full house according to Mother. I don't doubt that if her father had had any say in the matter the problem would have been solved. As it was, the cat was to go to the vet on the day of departure.

Whilst the van waited outside the front door the neighbours called again and again for Peter to come in, enticing him with saucer-rattling and a piece of fish. The cat struggled to respond to his mistress' entreaties, his sixth sense dormant, but he could not get free from the tight grip of Josie's little arms as she sat in an outside toilet clasping him to her bosom. The van drove off, Peter escaped his fate, and needless to say in due course there was another feline occupant of Josie's home where he soon enjoyed the comfortable existence that was the right of his kind, if they lived under the roof of a cat-lover.

Putting animals on the same level as human beings is for me going too far. Man is a supreme creature with an immortal soul. Pets, no matter how likeable, lovable, intelligent or domesticated, are creatures of the earth and should be treated as such.

We had not had time to improve our habitat much when the animal and a few sticks of furniture were kindly delivered, by Nora and Bert Wynn. Our circumstances had been explained to them and they were confident that Josie, at least, would give their pet a good home. I had to smile when Nora shook the cat's paw, said "Goodbye, Smokey, darling," and told him to be good.

III

He was a pretty little thing of the Persian type, with long white fur intermingled with grey, this undoubtedly explaining his name.

How dejected he looked as he sat on the floor with eyes shut and tail down. We stroked him and offered a saucer of milk and a piece of uncooked fish. He was not in the least bit interested. It was obvious he just wanted to be left alone in his private cat's world, so suddenly shattered by those large human creatures who had looked after him from his kittenhood and who had now deserted him. He looked, despite his despondency, a very young cat but was in fact two years old, a tom who had been neutered.

His whiskers were white, his nose pink and his eyes, when he deigned to open them for an instant, could be seen to be blue.

He was not very big and in relation to his body his head was small. He might, we thought, still grow. When I felt him I realised that he would have looked even more like a kitten were it not for his chief physical characteristic which was his fur. It was very thick, particularly around the cheeks, where it bunched off on either side, and on the underside of the belly. His markings made a distinctive pattern. Against the white background nature had placed them to advantage. The dark grey patches were around the ears sloping gently towards the front of the head and then upwards to the eyes. On the back they stopped short, then after white fur to the neckline, they recommenced and spread roughly in the pattern of a seagull in mid flight and facing away. Next came a further white section, then grey round the haunches tapering to points on either side. The darkest part of the cat was his long bushy tail.

Cats speak with their tails and reply to human language with motions like the rise and fall of a musical cadence. Smokey's tail now lay dejectedly on the floor. I lifted it up and it fell back without a sign of animation, a sure indication that Smokey was despondent.

"Shall we put butter on his paws, Josie?"

I had been told by plenty of people that this was the sure remedy for a desolate cat on being moved from one residence to another, the theory being that whilst the animal licked it off he gradually forgot his former home.

"Try it. At least it will give him something to do so that he won't notice his melancholia so much. You'll have to put him in the cupboard in the dark, poor thing."

This we did and he stayed there for an hour. When we hauled him out again from the exact spot we had put him, the butter was untouched. Josie sighed.

"Let's leave him alone. I'm sure he'll come round in time."

We left him sitting in the middle of the room beside his fish, milk and a newspaper with earth on it and made tracks for bed.

In the morning we found him under my bed with his eyes open and listening to the dawn chorus. Cats will adapt to most things and we felt sure that Smokey, too, would come to terms with his environment. We were loth to let him out before we had obtained a collar and name disc for him, but on the third day, which was Sunday, he got out anyway.

I was in the garden pulling out stinging nettles which were so high they obscured the light. Another season would have seen them up to the first floor.

Josie came out to tell me that lunch was ready. Smokey

seized his opportunity to escape by squeezing past her. Away he went at a brisk trot.

"He's off back to Balham," I said, remembering a cat my parents used to have who travelled twelve miles back to his old haunts, crossing a ferry on the way.

"Don't worry. He won't go far. I'm sure he's getting to like us."

She was probably right for he had been eating his food and there had been no reoccurrence of the sulks.

All that afternoon our concern showed itself by repeated looks out of the window and walks up and down the garden. As it grew towards evening we each took a portion of the street, knocked up the householders and asked if they had seen a white cat with grey markings. No one had. It was nearly dark and we decided to hope for the best that he would return of his own accord.

We left the back door open to make it easy for him and took one last look outside. Then I spotted him. He was sitting on the brick wall that divided our house from its semi-detached neighbour. The next door residence was still unsold.

We hurriedly devised a plan. I crept down to the bottom of the garden and slowly hoisted myself over a part of the wall which was lower than the rest. Having dropped quietly to the other side I made my way surreptitiously towards the cat. Josie, meanwhile, did her best to attract Smokey's attention by rattling a saucer. He took no notice of her, other than a slight turning of the head as if he just might be making up his mind about her. I did not take the chance that he might go to her but crept on up to him and slowly raising myself as he gazed in the other direction, grabbed him.

He offered no resistance and so I gently handed him

down the other side of the wall where Josie waited. She gratefully accepted and I sighed with relief.

Wonder of wonders - when I returned I found Smokey sitting on my wife's lap purring away as if he had not a care in the world. I could only conclude that it was a song of gratitude from his little cat mind that we had taken the trouble to find him and bring him in.

Further evidence that he was getting *au fait* with his new home was provided when he later spent a long time over the cat's ritual of cleaning himself with his tongue. Proof positive followed.

Josie and I had said goodnight to each other and settled down to sleep, leaving Smokey to continue his ablutions. There was the sound of a small animal jumping on my bed. Looking down I could just make out his little furry shape turning circles on the blankets - another typical feline habit that it is said dates back to his long distant past, when he lived in the wild and had to be wary of enemy intruders before retiring for the night.

As soon as we had obtained his collar and disc we fixed them on round his neck and felt a lot happier about things. We let him out when he wished to go - a small plaintive mew was the signal - and he returned when he was ready.

Now that we had a house complete with a cat we felt that was the end of the first stage of our endeavours. Much furnishing and fitting-up remained to be done but there was no sense of urgency any longer, only expectation.

We had obtained a second-hand armchair and chest of drawers, had been given an old, almost antique electric cooker and were looking forward to receiving our first visitors.

Josie's mother and father were known to all their children

as well as their nine grandchildren as Nana and Pop. They came by train from Luton, and arrived in time for Sunday lunch.

Suspecting that we might be finding the going rather rough they brought a chicken, already cooked. Pop also produced from a battered briefcase a bottle of *Entre-Deux-Mers* and two tins of cat food, ostensibly from the feline residents at his establishment, to Smokey. I think our cat would have preferred the chicken.

It was a pleasant day - the nearest we got to a house warming party.

"Yes," Pop said as he sipped a glass of the wine with a misty look in his eyes, "that creature – " indicating Smokey, "will do the same for you as Fifi did for me."

"How come?" I enquired.

Pop jerked his head towards Smokey again. "That animal has in full measure the cat's gift of being able to charm. Mark my words, he will worm his way into your hearts and stay there for ever."

"I think I'd rather like that," Josie said and I secretly smiled at my father-in-law.

"Maybe, my dear girl, maybe. I hope you have a splendid time together."

"I'm sure we will."

"I remember," said Pop, "once when Fifi was not much more than a kitten – "

Nana looked at us as if to say, 'He's off again'.

"Eat your food up," she commanded.

After lunch we strolled through Richmond and into Kew Gardens. The admission charge was so low - about one old penny each, if I remember aright - that Josie and I resolved to make it a regular Sunday morning jaunt, weather permitting.

There were already signs that Spring was on the way. A sprawling magnolia tree had its buds swelling and strange looking birds hopped occasionally out of the bushes.

"Go down to Kew in Lilac time," I quoted, but no one took any notice.

This was our first visit to the gardens and we were enraptured. We liked the pleasant, aimless ramble through the unspoilt, varied grounds, the tour round the glasshouse where exotic fruits grew on the trees, and the hothouse where a lily, as large as the room we lived in, floated luxuriously on the water.

By the time we got back to our house, there were only a few minutes to go before Nana and Pop had to leave. We were discussing the layout of our room and Nana made an odd observation.

"Look at that pattern on your floor," she said. "I do declare it's the shape of a horse's head."

She pointed the area out to us and there was no doubt that there was a darkish pattern on our bare boards that did look rather like the head of a horse. Looking at it more closely I was reminded of the knight piece used in Chess. Much conjecture was raised about the type of piece of furniture that might have stood there and accounted for the pattern.

"Anyway," I said, "by the time you next come down we will have covering on the floor. We will move into the front room, use this as the kitchen-cum-dining room."

"Getting civilised at last," Nana said, and chuckled.

We thought we had better get a move on with putting the

place to rights, for one morning there had come a knock on the front door. Upon opening it we had been confronted by a woman who said she had seen the advertising board had been taken away, but as the house still appeared empty, was it being put back on the market? We explained as best we could but she plainly doubted us, though why she should I do not know.

At the first available opportunity we made a trip to Clapham Junction, which we had been told was a cheap shopping area. We purchased a roll of floor covering at a bargain price, and net and velvety curtains. The substitute lino was for the back room and the curtains for the front.

Before cutting out the floor covering I discovered by chance a game that Smokey (and I, too) could enjoy. I had an old table tennis ball and found that if I rolled it through the lino, Smokey would wait at the other end for it to appear and then smartly knock it back to me with a paw. The cat appeared to get mild amusement out of this, rather than excitement or satisfaction. Unfortunately, there was work to be done.

Being completely without experience, I found it a long and tedious job, but at least I made only minor mistakes. When the job was done, I surveyed it with pride and was glad that 'the horse's head' had gone. Josie, meanwhile, was sewing rings on the main curtains, having quickly put up the ready-made net ones.

Things were going well and we invited Nana and Pop down again, this time insisting that they were not to bring food with them. Nana was a heavy woman and when she stomped about could be heard at the other end of the house. Naturally she wanted to give a hand with the lunch preparations.

I was in the front room nattering to Pop, Josie was having

a bath and Smokey was in the garden. We heard a crash and rushing out to the kitchen found Nana on the floor. Fortunately, she wasn't hurt, but it was mortifying to see the state of the floor covering I had so assiduously laid. Where she had gone down, the floor boards had snapped and left a gaping rent. What had happened was that as she had trotted around, one of her feet had suddenly gone through the lino and also the floor beneath, causing her to trip. I examined the area.

By pulling back the floor-covering, I was able to do a makeshift repair with a large piece of hardboard and tacks. The incident depressed me and I wondered what the rest of the floor was like, and were the other rooms any better - or worse? It was our own fault. We should have had the house surveyed instead of letting our enthusiasm get the better of commonsense.

Spring was early that year and it soon passed into summer as we continued with our efforts. Sunday was the one day of the week when substantial progress could be made on renovation and improvement. The old-fashioned windows needed new sash cords. There were wardrobes to be erected in the corners of the front room for us to hang up our clothes in, instead of leaving them strewn around in carriers. Electric points were needed all over the place, for the Electricity Board had given us a new meter with a high capacity.

There was, unfortunately, a great lack of money, bearing in mind that there were two mortgages that had to be paid, and rates and other overheads to be accounted for. Josie obtained a Sundays-only job as a waitress in Kew Gardens' restaurant. This left me to concentrate on speedily doing all that was desired on the house, with the bare minimum of tools and my somewhat inadequate knowledge. However, I found it amazing what I could do when I found I had to, instead of sending out for a builder and spending money!

One morning I looked at a door that needed a lock and wondered how I could possibly accomplish the job. I was competent and confident in only one respect, the wiring of the place, for I had an excellent electrical knowledge and this must have saved us many pounds.

There was a small lobby between the front and back rooms of the house and during an afternoon I was going from one to the other when I pulled up short, as something caught my eye on the front room door. About half-way up the lintels of the door was an orange object about three inches in diameter. I was completely at a loss to understand what it was and examined it with great curiosity. I got a stick and poked it, discovering that it was soft like rubber. Then I noticed that on the floor spreading in all directions was what to all intents and purposes was brown dust and this heightened my perplexity. Although I thought long and hard about it I eventually came to a completely wrong conclusion.

It was a rather cruel inference though it made sense to me. Josie was to blame! It was her job to keep the house in reasonably clean and tidy order. That did not mean she had to scrub the floors and clean the woodwork every day, but she must have so neglected her duties that dust had accumulated. So much so that not only did it lay spread out on the floor, but it had settled in every available spot for so long that plants had been allowed to sprout. When she returned from Kew Gardens, I roundly upbraided her.

"Just look at it," I said, pointing to the floor and the horrible orange thing that faced us. "I know we've been busy but I would have thought that you had time to do a little once a week to keep the place from being overgrown. Aren't you ashamed you've let things so go?"

Poor Josie, apart from being rightly annoyed at my

outburst, was as mystified as I had been, but was convinced it was not her fault. It was one of those moments when, whatever else may be said about them, a cigarette acts like a good Samaritan. When we had calmed down, Josie cleared her throat and spoke.

"There's something else."

"What?"

"Don't jump down my throat again."

"No, no. I won't. What is it? What is it?"

"The horse's head is back!"

We rushed out to the kitchen and there, sure enough, was the unmistakable pattern showing on the lino, just as it had appeared on the bare boards. I'll swear it was grinning.

"You should have told me before."

"I didn't want to worry you."

"Never mind. The point is, what is it? I shall have to make a thorough examination of the house and only hope that the whole lot doesn't fall down while I'm doing it. Where's Smokey?"

"In the garden, I expect."

"Good. Keep him out of the way as I go round. I don't want him disappearing beneath the foundations."

The top of the house, which remained unoccupied, was as it had been when we moved in - bare on floor and ceiling and with the pretty wall-papered walls showing in contrast.

The ground floor was dreadful. Mostly where I looked there was brown dust. The wainscot in both rooms was badly warped and in some places coming away from the wall. The underside of the lino was a mass of white fibrous threads and there was a dank, musty smell emanating. Large cracks were on the floorboards and the hardboard I had tacked down was loose.

The most disturbing discovery was that of other growths in one corner. Unlike the first they looked like snails, asleep and waiting to resume a crawl upwards. I was depressed at the conclusion of my search and my joke was feeble.

"We've been invaded by Martians. They're all set to conquer the earth."

"I do wish they had started somewhere else. What are we going to do?"

"I just don't know. Let's not panic but give the matter a good long think."

Having pondered for hours I came to the inescapable conclusion that the timbers of the house were rotten through and through. As to the answer to the problem I had none except that we would have to call in experts who would charge us lots of hard-earned cash. I decided that a further day or so would make little difference. A postponement of a decision might give us a solution, if there was one. In the meantime we did what we could.

I removed the ugly fungus from the lintel of the porch door and from the wainscot, cutting into it with a penknife and scraping underneath as bits of rotten wood flaked away. We moved all of our possessions to the floor above, including food, then went over every bit of the downstairs walls and floors with strong disinfectant. The cat did not mind the changed circumstances. We fell asleep exhausted.

The following evening I went to the library on Richmond Green and borrowed books on wood decay and preservation. I sat reading them till well after midnight and gained considerable enlightenment, but it was not reassuring. We were suffering from wood rot. I could not decide whether it was of the wet or dry variety. This was apparently due to air holes being blocked up, long neglect and dampness seeping into the wood. From the accounts I read, it was a common trouble with old houses that had not been properly looked after and could also occur in new dwellings if they were left undisturbed for a lengthy time without occupation.

After a search I found the air-blocks and the holes were clogged with dirt and muck. I unblocked them and hoped that I had got at the root of the trouble. Next I took up our so recently laid floor-covering, tore it up into small pieces and put them in the dustbin. It was an easy job to pull up a floorboard here and there so as to discover the extent of the damage. It was considerable.

The front room was not affected save for the area near the porch door where swellings on the wainscot indicated to me that the rot had advanced that far. They would have to be replaced. It did not take me long to decide that the lobby and the back room were write-offs. The conclusion was inevitable. The builders would have to be brought in and whatever estimate they gave would have to be accepted.

Ah, well. The house was cheap and once the second mortgage had been paid off, it would not be so bad.

The Richmond and Twickenham Times had many advertisements from local builders who specialised in the treatment of floors like ours and we rang them up. Of the three who turned up we were particularly impressed with a young fellow who, from the way he talked, could have been a throw-back to the yeomanry of Anglo-Saxon days. His independent approach to life was refreshing and we were not surprised to learn that he had left his father's old-established business and had branched out on his own account.

He gave the area a thorough going over, prodding here and there, whistling with surprise occasionally and saying at regular intervals, "Yes, Guv. You've got a problem here, right enough, but not to worry."

His verdict was short: "Dry rot, Guv. You've got a problem here but not to worry."

The whole of the floor and wainscot would have to be taken up including the joists, the area scourged minutely with a blow lamp, fungicide applied to the brickwork and the floor relaid with concrete. The wood would have to be taken away and burnt. I asked him why we could not burn the wood ourselves and he informed me that it was taking too big a risk. If the fumes went up the chimney, or even found their way in from outside there was a chance that reinfection could happen in the upper reaches. I was amazed.

"How much will it cost?"

"Don't worry about that, Guv. I've worked it out that I can do the whole lot for a hundred and fifty which will give me the margin I want. Don't mention the cost to me again. I don't like figures. I'll do a good job and I shall have to be paid within a week of completion. When will that be, Guv, you're asking. Give me three weeks so that I can get some boys together and that'll be it."

"Will you be submitting a written estimate?"

"No, Guv. I don't worry about them things. It's a hundred and fifty and it won't vary."

I thought it was very cheap but was so struck by the transparent honesty of the man that I immediately accepted.

The charge was a heavy one to us in our prevailing financial condition, but very cheap indeed to what we had expected. With adjustments here and there we could manage it. Once again it was a case of having to.

I was doubtful about the three weeks quoted but Jack was

as good as his word. A few days' later he arrived back with three colleagues and they worked with great gusto, tearing up the floor and carting the rotten wood out to an open van in which it was taken away to be disposed of. Jack and another mate did the blowlamp work.

A week later the gang was back again with sand and cement. After a lavish scour-out with an evil smelling fluid, the major part of the operation took place. They certainly worked, shovelling in the hardcore followed by the cement which was applied in stages. The final layer was carefully smoothed out and we were told to let it sweat.

Precisely to the day Jack came back, examined the finished job and pronounced himself satisfied. So were we. It was the end of a traumatic experience that had caused us sleepless nights. When Jack arrived to collect his money we were so pleased that we offered him twenty pounds more than he had asked for. It was a gesture we could ill afford but we felt it had to be made. True to his rough-cut basic Englishman's instincts, Jack refused.

"No, Guv. Don't you worry. You keep it. I quoted the price and got my margin and that's all there is to it."

An admirable person who commanded respect. I wish there were more like him about. We had to leave the concrete a further week to sweat and then had a perfect new floor to walk on.

One evening when Josie was out I took a piece of chalk and, going over to the appropriate position, drew on the concrete a large green horse's head.

"He's friendly now," I said.

Smokey had taken the whole operation in his stride, accepting tit-bits from the men when they had their lunch and looking on with interest as they worked away. He probably appreciated the company during the day.

We had not wasted the enforced interval but had continued to work on other parts of the house. Our progress was often laborious because of the necessity to travel to the West End to do rather uninteresting tasks, but we were grateful for the financial rewards that we could plough back into the house. Often, however, after a day spent travelling and working with the added frustrations of overcrowded tube trains and badly ventilated offices, we would crawl into our beds tired out.

There was one particular job that gave me much satisfaction. The door leading from the front room to the lobby had escaped vital damage despite the happening of that awful Sunday. The lintel, however, was crumbling and I had the task of replacing it and re-fixing the door. I had learned something from Jack and went over the area with a blow lamp, placed a new post duly impregnated with a paraffin liquid in position, gave it iron supports and put the door back. Encouraged thus I did the same with the kitchen door.

Just in case some of the white tendrils had found their way upstairs, I soaked each room with wood preservative. When Operation Overkill, as I called it, was over we at last relaxed.

We must have had a mania for work in those days, but we did manage to indulge in a few pleasant walks by the river, strolls to Kew and Twickenham and, what we enjoyed most of all, the shows at Richmond Theatre.

IV

Cats are perverse creatures. Now that the shouting, the hammering and the sound of mixing concrete were over, Smokey began to act oddly. Perhaps it was because we could not look after him as much as he would have liked, or maybe the scent of freedom had got up his nostrils, but the fact was that when we let him out in the morning, he would take one look at us and go galloping across the garden wall.

This, by itself, was all right and we were glad that he was able to lead an independent life of his own as all cats should. He had on his name tag, so, if by chance he got lost we hoped the finder would return him to us.

The trouble was that the freedom appeared to go to his head. Long after we had returned from our places of work there would be no sign of him and when dusk fell we would get anxious. Usually he appeared at the last moment on the garden wall where he would wait, listening to our cajoling and darting off if we attempted to pick him up. Once he was in of his own accord he would settle down on a lap and purr with contentment.

To look at his countenance to see if there was some sign there of what he wanted was exasperating. His basic nature was placid, but there must have been a playful imp in him somewhere.

We became crafty with him, feeding him only at night and this method of getting at him through his stomach worked on the whole. His running wild was a nuisance.

Most cats like to assume the domestic role of their own free will and Smokey was no exception, though he carried it to the extreme.

Other subtle feline characteristics that I have noticed

include sitting in the darkness gazing at the moon and the stars with wonder on their little faces, listening to the trees rustling gently, and hearing noises not detectable by the human ear. They love to adopt the alert stance too, to be ready to take action against dangers, real or imagined. Smokey had all these traits finely honed and appeared to glory in them.

No cat is worth its salt if it gives no trouble at all and no pet owner should take on the responsibility of looking after a cat or a dog if they are not prepared to put up with the snags.

I think we were patient enough. The biggest headache he gave us was his fur. It was luxurious and that was the trouble. It was a shame that such lovely fur, so soft to the touch, should get matted, which it often did.

Every couple of weeks we had the task of giving him a thorough brushing and cutting out of lumps of matted fur, particularly from his stomach, where it formed large tufts that he vainly tried to chew off himself. It was a painstaking operation for one had to be very careful in case he gave a jerk or other sudden movement. Josie declared that if she saved all the wool she cut off him, she would eventually have enough to make a scarf.

Another annoyance was that malady that most cats and dogs suffer from to a lesser or great degree - fleas. For all his licking and biting, Smokey could not rid himself of these pests and we had, therefore, to get powder and massage it in. This he took as an affront to his dignity for we had to hold him for ten minutes whilst the powder did its work and he could not be allowed to lick before the powder was brushed out. Smokey hated the whole operation and when the session was over would creep under a chair and stare moodily at us.

During his wild phase, Smokey became a thief. We had

brought home mince meat for him and left it in its bag in the middle of a table. When our backs were turned he had contrived to get the wrapping off and had eaten most of it before we caught him in the act.

He knew it was against the rules to get on the table and I gave him a sharp slap on his haunches, which punishment did not prevent him having another go on a subsequent occasion.

In some odd way we had got into the habit of leaving the 'S' out of his name when addressing him. It is doubtful if Mokey noticed the difference but he certainly got to know the sound of our voices and their different inflections. He could tell when his name was mentioned if we were talking to each other.

Certain phrases, also, stuck in his memory-banks, such as when we had food for him and said, in a suitable high-pitched voice, "Is this what you want?" Also the word 'fish', which we applied to any type of food, impinged on him so that when he heard the word uttered in another context, he would come over and expect something.

I would not say he was a particularly intelligent cat, rather one that was quick on the uptake. His ears would prick up instantly at anything that referred to him or interested him in any way. The biggest problem of all with him turned out to be another cat.

It was a real devil of an animal but I suppose his owner thought the world of him. It was a large black and white creature with long whiskers and a tail that swished to and fro whenever we saw him. In fact, he was rather on the lines of Sylvester of the Tweetie Pie cartoon fame. That is what we called him - Sylvester. As far as we could ascertain he was the only other cat in the neighbourhood. If this was so, it was natural that he should turn his attentions on our little animal, but unfortunately they were decidedly nefarious.

Smokey would be sitting on the wall and Sylvester would sneak up on him from behind and jump on him. He did not bite or scratch but there would be a struggle and Mokey always got the worst of it. When we got him in after such an encounter he would stand cowering and needed a lot of reassurance before submitting to be examined. His back fur would be in an appalling condition, covered with mess and smelling dreadfully.

To Josie would fall the task of cleaning him up with warm water and mild disinfectant. It was a well nigh impossible job for him to do on his own, for he would be in a hideous state and it would have taken him ages. Nor did we like to think of him licking such a large amount of mess, the smell meanwhile persisting.

Things came to a head when one evening he persisted in going out. He had not been gone two minutes before we heard his anguished cries and he slunk in looking as if he had come out of a swamp and smelling like it.

Josie gave him a scolding and I followed it up with a slap and much shouting. I was disgusted with him for, if Sylvester was the villain of the piece, Smokey was a contributory agent by going into the danger area merely because he wanted to be outside after having been given full range for the whole of the day.

After his punishment, Smokey sat on the floor looking at me with a puzzled expression on his little face and I supposed he could not understand why his kind master should chastise him after the event. With a final shout at him I went into the other room and lay on the bed to read a newspaper.

After a few moments I heard a slight noise and glancing up saw that Mokey had entered and jumped on the bed as if nothing untoward had recently occurred. He was gazing at me and having gained my attention he stood looking at me expectantly. I smiled, for the last thing I had expected to see was him in a good mood. He stood there for a while just gazing at me as I looked amusedly back at him. He then made up his mind and with long purposeful steps advanced along the bed and brushed aside the newspaper.

The cat was undoubtedly a strange one to so soon forget his chastisement and where it had come from for, imagine my astonishment when he thrust his little face into mine and planted a cat's kiss on my lips.

I call it a cat's kiss. He ran his mouth and whiskers along my lips and then looked up into my eyes with a hopeful look on his face.

Even the hardest of hearts would have melted. Smokey was so obviously saying one or both of two things - 'I am sorry for all the trouble I've caused,' 'I forgive you for what you did.' As I gently stroked him and he settled down on my chest uttering a paean of happiness, I knew then that Pop was right. He had wormed his way into my heart.

Of course, he was unable to understand that roaming the garden on his own, doing exactly as he pleased but unable to defend himself against a creature like Sylvester, was stupid no matter how fresh the air was. The problem of protecting him from the devil cat had to be solved some other way. I resolved he could keep his freedom though it would require more time and work from his two human friends.

We built him a cage. Not a small rabbit hutch structure but an enclosure that stretched from the bars of the scullery window, past the shed with the grass hump on it, into the garden proper. I acquired yards of wire netting, staples and stakes. When it was all done, Smokey was able to have his freedom to go in and out as he wished, to breathe the fresh air and to gaze at the moon to his heart's content, and the nearest Sylvester could get to him was the other side of the wire.

The basic essential restriction on him was that he could not go deep into the garden or over the walls, as cats so love to do. Thus would be his life from Mondays to Fridays and at night, but when we were there in the daytime he roamed as before and we kept our eyes open for the approach of Sylvester.

Yet on the first day we returned from work, arriving by chance at our house at the same time, he was nowhere to be seen. There was a simple explanation. I noticed a lump on the bed that was moving upwards and Smokey emerged from the sheets blinking in the light. Very soon he settled down to the life of a domesticated cat and yearned no more for the mad rambles of the back gardens, and we turned our attention again to the house.

After the thorough disinfection of the rooms, the hanging of the curtains, the laying of the lino and the fitting of shelves, points and cupboards, furniture was installed. Some of it was second-hand and some was bought on hire-purchase and none of it was luxurious. We did not, as yet, possess a television, a refrigerator, or a washing machine, but were working towards these things. A door-to-door salesman got us to invest in a vacuum cleaner which was a bit unnecessary as the only carpeting was on the stairs. When we had pictures on the walls the house could almost be termed a home and was certainly presentable to visitors, few and far between though they might be.

The bathroom was one of the remaining obstacles to the completion of a home fit to live in. It was in a very poor state and not a task I fancied doing myself. We therefore obtained estimates from various decorators, but these were much too high for us, so once again it was a case of saving money and spending time.

We had now been at our house for four months and had got to know the town somewhat. Richmond was very much a community on its own. The two bridges at either end of the main dwelling and shopping area marked the western boundaries with Twickenham and beyond. The Kew Road rolled away till it reached Kew Bridge. To the south lay the suburb within a suburb of Ham, and the east stretched towards London. Where it merged with the great metropolis, it became lost in postal numbers and its identity was diluted, save where the hill culminating in the view and the great park held sway.

There were many local clubs and societies catering for all types and ages and we determined to take an active part in the affairs of the community when we were ready, but for the time being our walks by the river and visits to the theatre continued to be our main relaxations.

We had also acquired delivery of a much belated wedding present from my mother and father and considering its many years of neglect, the Brinsmead piano was in reasonably good condition. My parents had held on to this whilst we were in rooms and must have despaired of us ever being able to receive it. It arrived early one morning and came in through the front window.

Neither of us could play although as a child I had had some rudimentary instruction from my mother, who, at the time, had been taking lessons herself. This instrument had been the cause of a major family rift in our home and as I tapped out the odd tune here and there, I was pleased that the piano had found pride of place at last in our front room. One day, surely, it would come into its own. Mokey soon discovered it and would walk up and down the keys amusing us and puzzling him.

As the summer moved towards autumn, we debated whether we could afford a holiday and if so what was to become of the cat. We had grown fond of him and the thought of putting him in a pet's boarding home did not appeal.

We had neighbours on the detached side of us, but as yet had only spoken a few words to them, certainly not enough to justify asking them to do us a favour which would involve some effort on their part. Indeed, we had only glimpsed the old man in his porch doorway once. His wife had pleasantly wished us good morning four or five times and we hoped that later on we would get to know her better. As for the other side, it remained obstinately empty.

The answer was simple - Nana and Pop. Two such cat lovers, if willing and available, would soon muck in with Smokey. A telephone call confirmed that Nana would be delighted to spend a week at Richmond and Pop would be able to come down at the weekends to assist.

"I'll miss him," Josie said.

"We're only going for seven days, you know, and he'll be in the best of hands. So good, in fact, that the question is, will he miss us, and will it be a good miss?"

"I'm sure it will not be the same thing for him. He's a sensitive cat and will probably go off his food."

We booked up for the very cheapest package holiday possible which was a week at Ostend, semi-pension, and included entertainment and a trip to Brussels.

Mokey knew something was going on when he saw our cases on the floor. He looked at them, sniffed them and sat on them, then looked happily at us as if to say we were not to worry.

The night before we departed, having already posted the

keys to Nana, we made out a list of requests and instructions, attaching to them a day-by-day menu for Smokey. Outside it was stormy, the latest culmination in what had been a poor summer even by English standards. We worked to the accompaniment of the noise of heavy rainfall.

What with one thing and another, in getting the house clean and making ready ourselves, we rather overdid it and went to bed at half past three, preparatory to getting up again at eight. Josie maintained that it wasn't worth going to bed at all and the fact that we did made the getting up more difficult.

Having said farewell to Mokey - shades of his arrival - - we made our way to the station and caught the tube to Victoria. We had time to spare when we got there and decided to look up our old bed-sitter house, the place where we had dreamed and planned, and where, despite the prevailing money-grabbing image of landlords, ours had been so genial. He had been a foreigner - Greek, I think - and his rough but kindly advice given to us on countless occasions had been, "Don't 'rust nobody."

We had reserved seats which had been a condition of the purchase of the tickets. I went aboard the London-to-Dover train and found the conditions chaotic. Josie, meanwhile, being unaware of this went off to get magazines and chocolate.

Every carriage was jammed tight with passengers and after a search I found our carriage and seats. They were occupied. Two large women who from their conversation I judged to be German, lay back smoking cigarettes and to my polite request to them to move, returned a blank stare. I showed them our reservation slips to no avail and a kindly fellow passenger translated my request, but the blank stare remained. They were obviously not going to shift and it was impossible given the circumstances to find a guard. I was getting concerned, too, that Josie had not arrived on the scene.

I glared at the German hausfrauen and shouted at them in English. They glared back and clutched their handbags more tightly. I looked out of the window and on the crowded platform people were rushing to and fro trying to find room to get on. I could just see the guard's raised green flag before I heard his whistle and the train began to move. Then I spotted Josie who was haring down the platform. I waved and opened the door, just managing to pull her on before the train gathered speed.

Quickly I explained the situation to her and she endeavoured to communicate with the Germans with no more success than I had had. Having had only a few hours' sleep and feeling tired and dishevelled, I was close to losing my temper and by now other passengers had joined in the attempt to shift the women, who uttered not a word between them the whole time. Fortunately, a scoutmaster, who was escorting a group of scouts, calmed all concerned, particularly me. Short of using physical force and that would not have been easy, there was nothing more we could do so we stood all the way to Dover and grumbled at our appalling start to the holiday.

Yes, Josie had nearly not made it. Having made her purchases she had returned to the barrier to be told by an official that the train was full up and no-one else was to be allowed on the platform. In vain she had told him that she had her ticket and a reserved seat and that I was on the train with the luggage. Frantically, with only seconds to spare she had ducked under his arms and raced up to my receding carriage. That had so nearly been the start and end of our holiday.

The train was forgotten as we stood on the deck of the König Albert, save for an image of flooded fields in which sad-eyed cows and horses stood motionless. We queued for drinks, then inched ourselves round the ship and found a couple of wooden seats available. Almost too weary to eat our sandwiches, we soon dozed off, but it was a very short forty winks before we aroused ourselves to the clanking of chains, the noise of hooters and the bustle of the crew as they prepared to tie up at the Ostend quayside.

We grabbed our bags and took in the first impressions. Cranes and ships, porters and foreign spelling. Two couriers awaited us, one of either sex and they both welcomed us in perfect English. They escorted us through the customs without bother and so on to a mini-bus that sped through the flag bedecked streets.

I could hardly believe we had left London, for the hotels and shops we passed had a good variety of British names - The Shakespeare, The Brighton and even The Richmond. We were put off at a hotel that could not have been more English-named - The Blackpool - located in The Rue de Royale, subtitled Koningsstraat, translated by us as King's Road.

"Voila!"

Our host and hostess at the hotel introduced themselves to us as John and Marguerite, hoped we had had a pleasant trip, and then got us to sign the register. Before taking us to our rooms they asked to have our passports, a formality that I accepted rather doubtfully though they assured us they would be returned on the morrow. A maid took our bags and we all trooped up to the third floor.

We had a view of coloured roof tops, jumbled together continental style, trees in the background and ivy on the walls in the close-at-hand back gardens.

There were two beds in the room, one large and one small. This pleased us for we preferred to sleep singly and

Josie grabbed the larger. The simple set-up was completed by a basin with hot and cold taps, a wardrobe, a chest of drawers and a pair of easy chairs.

We washed and went down to a room which was half a lounge and half a diner. There were eight tables, six of which were occupied and we took our places opposite a young Scottish couple. The maid, a pretty dark haired girl called Ginette, wheeled in a trolley and served soup from a large tureen. It was a tasty mixture of onions, tomatoes and a few other things, with a faint trace of garlic. The main course was haslet salad, and for sweet a fresh pear.

The pot of tea that rounded off the meal was disappointing, particularly as we were addicts.

A notice placed on each table and printed in four languages intrigued us, though what it stated was innocuous enough, i.e. that drunkenness was forbidden.

After dinner we surprisingly felt active enough to go for a walk and exploration of the resort. It just had to be a little different from Brighton, and it was.

The sea was only a minute's stroll away and it fronted a wide sandy beach, which in turn gave way to a narrow promenade, directly behind which was the area of hotels, shops and cafés. We bought ice creams with our francs and sniffed the ozone.

The town itself was full with visitors, most of them English, and the bakers shops were very tempting with their displays of continental and exotic looking pastries. Avenues of fairy lights enhanced the holiday atmosphere which was geared, without a doubt, to the British market. The picture postcards, though, were rude enough to make even the most outlandish south-east coast resort colour up a little.

The souvenirs consisted almost solely of a play upon a single character, a little boy fashioned in everything from a corkscrew to a barometer, with all possible variations in between. The boy was depicted doing what is only normally done in private. His rudeness was perplexing in that it was extolled as a virtue.

We managed to get lost for half-an-hour but soon located the sea again, from whence it was an easy matter to trace our route back to the Rue de Royale. Actually we passed it twice but noted only the German name of Koningsstraat. It was about time they took it down - that reminder of the occupation.

We had hoped to sleep but the weather deteriorated again. The lightning flashed and the thunder roared and being in a strange room did not help.

I have always been something of an insomniac, working on the principle that one poor night's rest will be made up for by the next, but I had only to look at my wife to see that she had a different constitution. The bags under her eyes told their story.

I took her an early tea at seven o'clock, which I had brewed with the aid of a small solid fuel heater and kettle we had brought with us, and went out for a solitary saunter along the beach. The weather had at last changed for the better and it was really nice to see the sun shining from a cloudless sky. When I came back to our room I found that Josie had fallen asleep again with the tea still in the cup, but the gong was going so I roused her.

"A continental breakfast awaits you," I said.

"A what? Oh, yes. I wonder how Mokey's getting on."

"Doing well with your doting parents, I expect, and hoping we're away for a month. I wish we were, too."

It was a good first day. After the standard croissant roll and butter with watery coffee, a chat with the Scottish couple, a sit-down on a park bench beside a garrulous Flemish lady (made interesting by our mutual ignorance of each other's language), lunch of fish and chips and a round of crazy golf, one could shut one's eyes and imagine one was in Margate. That may not have been exciting but it was relaxing. At one hole of the crazy golf we laughed at a German couple who, misreading a notice that had been overgrown by weeds, took the word 'paiser' to be 'baiser' and exuberantly kissed each other.

Ostend was a town of bands. First we discovered one in a bandstand heartily playing a selection from Madame Butterfly, then having moved on we found a procession led by a youth band churning out Lili Marlene. We chased it for a while, took photographs, turned into another street and saw advancing towards us a third orchestra. This was certainly different from the average for each musician was riding a bicycle. Their rhythm was excellent.

We bought several picture postcards and decided to go to the casino of which we had heard. Unfortunately when we got there we were informed that we could not go in as we were not members and there were too many formalities to be observed.

"Just as well," Josie remarked as we made our way back to the hotel. "There's no knowing what you would have done with our money."

"Most probably I would have won us a fortune and next year we could go to the south of France."

The week went very quickly. On Monday there was a coach tour of Ostend, on which we were told it was the anniversary of their liberation. We were shown a large area of wasteland that had once been the site of the largest hotel in the town - The Palace - unfortunately burnt to the ground during the war.

Tuesday was the great day. A visit to Brussels and the World Fair.

"If you love Paris," our guide announced, "Brussels is like having tea with the loved one's sister."

Charlie, as he was called, passed the journey with similar witticisms. The autobahn was straight and monotonous.

We saw so many sights that day, including the statue of Leopold commemorating the founding in 1831 of the Belgian nation, and the house where Byron had completed his Childe Harold epic. However, the one that attracted our attention the most, by reason of the hundreds who milled around to get a glimpse of it, was a monument to the little boy who we had seen on the picture postcards and souvenirs in the Ostend stores.

Having threaded our way to the clicking of many cameras past cars and coaches, we came to the edge of the crowd and craned our necks. It took us many minutes more to get close enough to read the inscription on the fountain-stone. MANAKIN-PIS (1690). So the meaning of Belgium's national hero long turned into a shrine to laughter became clear - almost - and like everyone else, we smiled.

The World Fair fully lived up to its reputation and our only regret was that we could not spend a whole day there. We managed to visit the American, Russian and British pavilions as well as two others, concluding our trip with a top to bottom tour of The Atomium, a curious structure of spheres and connecting staircases.

Wednesday night was that of the candlelight social where the British let their hair down, and where Josie, a somewhat larger than average girl, all but gave a small chap a hernia in a mock wheel-barrow race.

On Thursday we went on our own to Bruges, and saw its canals, quaint streets, the Béguinage that displayed the notice in several languages: 'Please do not photograph the Nuns' and the Brangwyn Exhibition.

On Friday we went shopping for souvenirs. We bought a huge cigar for John and a box of chocolates for Marguerite. This was a consolation and an apology for having burnt a small hole in the carpet of our room when boiling up tea the previous night and about which they had been most understanding. At last we had a brief time to sit on the beach, swim a little in the warm sea, look out at the ships and feel the heat of the sun on our bodies. As we looked northwards to England we agreed that after a dodgy start it had been a most enjoyable little holiday, particularly so, I fancy, because we had been so in need of it.

The ship departed considerably earlier than anticipated which must have disappointed a couple from the hotel who were to wave goodbye. The boat was not nearly so crowded as on the outward trip, so we were able to get our duty-free cigarettes, spirits and wine in comfort, and also have a meal in the restaurant.

Without a hitch we were back on the train speeding towards The Smoke and Smokey.

"He has been a very good boy," Nana said. "Didn't want to go out much and explored every room a dozen times. Looking for you, I expect."

Cats seldom have the instant recognition facility that dogs possess. Smokey sniffed the luggage for several minutes before deciding the issue by jumping on Josie's lap and looking up at her. Soon he was purring and pawing his pleasure that she was back. Yes, it was, at Josie remarked, good to be *en famille* again. That night he slept on my bed after his week on a chair.

V

At long last there were people in the house next door and the board was down. Unlike us they had quickly put up curtains and we could hear sounds of activity - the whirring of a vacuum cleaner and conversation against the background of a television. Smokey pricked up his ears and went to his window. We wondered if they had dry rot.

There was a distinct touch of autumn about. Leaves drifted onto the front door mat, the nights were drawing in and there was that indefinable atmosphere akin to the time of the year. It was hard to believe that nearly a year had passed since we had first viewed our home and that we were now looking forward to our first Christmas there.

The dawn chorus no longer roused us from sleep and we were used to looking out at greenery, instead of Victoria's concrete buildings from which, in the distance, neon signs had glowed. Such is acclimatisation.

I do not know how it started, but a ritual we now engaged in was table tennis with the cat. That's what we called it and it became a regular feature of our evenings.

We would clear the room of furniture, produce a ping-pong ball and in would trot Mokey. He would sit down demurely at one end of the room washing himself. Now and then he cast a quick glance in our direction as we rolled the ball to one another, waiting for the chance that one of us would send it in his direction. As the ball approached him he would take no notice until it was almost up to him, then lash out with a paw and send the ball careering towards us. Sometimes he varied his play by making out he was taking a cat nap and at other times, impatient to be brought into the game, he would tap a paw on the floor. He never chased the ball, being content for us to do the retrieving, and so it would continue.

We had tried other methods of keeping him amused and happy without much success, such as a clockwork mouse, a cotton reel and a tennis ball, but Mokey preferred his ping--pong. Like most cats, however, he had a love of wool and many was the time he got himself entangled and would chew through the wool to get free.

We thought that perhaps he was a lonely animal and wondered if the introduction of a kitten would give him the companionship he lacked during the day. I remembered, however, that my mother had once taken in a young cat for the same reason and the result had been disastrous.

Her own pet had so taken umbrage that he had refused to enter his home again and had to be fed outside. Nor had he relented when the new cat had been passed on to someone else. It had taken many weeks for him to be coaxed in again, where he had died a few days afterward from, as my mother said, a broken heart.

Certainly Mokey was a good companion to us. He became slowly but surely, and without any conscious effort on his or our part, a kind of link with the circumstances that existed; us, him and the house.

It could be said that it had been so from the beginning and this is true in the sense that we fed and sheltered him, but a cat's nature is basically independent. He will often accept (or refuse) what is given him and go away and lead his own life. Mokey gradually lost that part of his nature.

He was not slavish like a dog, but as things had turned out and he had found himself with us, he decided after a due interval that it was more than just a good thing. He would throw in his lot with us so that we could all three together lead a reasonable life.

A bit of luck for him and us occurred in that Sylvester's owner left the district and the cage and cat-run became more or less redundant, but Mokey continued to use it if he wanted to go out at night and he did not run wild again when he had his freedom every day of the week.

He took it in turns which bed he slept on, a doubtful honour for us as it effected some discomfort. He had changed his place from the bottom of the bed to a position half way up on the side, so whoever had him had to be careful that he or she did not accidentally throw him off in the middle of the night. It did happen now and then but he would return and cosily coil up in the same spot.

A cat's mind is small, but to judge from the enquiring look we often observed in Mokey's eyes, he did use what he had. He sometimes sat for minutes looking at us as much as to say, 'Now what are they up to?' He also focused them on other things that interested him - a new object in the home, an aeroplane passing overhead, a bee buzzing about in its search for pollen, or a fly on the window. He had the cat's love of hunting, stalking small insects on the ground and once or twice a field mouse came within his grasp.

He did not eat them but brought them in and laid them before us. If the creature, still alive, attempted to escape, he would fetch it back and allow us to take it from his mouth and dispose of it. On these occasions we would reward him with a morsel of food, hoping, meanwhile, that his victim had gone where he could not be found again - there, perhaps, to recover, or die in peace.

Our garden was not particularly big, but large enough to be managed with an effort and it must have had good soil, for peas, tomatoes and rhubarb all flourished without a lot of attention. We were fortunate, too, that next door's garden had a large apple tree in it and most of the branches hung over our side of the wall.

The amount of cooking apples we collected from the ground was enough to supply us with our needs for many months. We had only one thing against that tree. When in full leaf, it effectively hid from view the pagoda in Kew Gardens, an embellishment, when visible, that delighted us.

It was agreed that Nana and Pop would spend Christmas with us and that they would supply the turkey. When the bird was brought in Mokey was at his most inquisitive. He could hardly believe his eyes and when it was hung up in the pantry, he sat down and stared at the door with an intrigued look. We felt sure he was working out ways to find a favourable moment for gaining access, or whether he could get up on his hind legs and release the catch.

Knowing the perversity of cats I was not surprised that when the moment came and the bird was on the table ready to be eaten, he refused his tit-bits. Perhaps it was because we had pilchards in tomato sauce in the house which was his favourite repast. At any rate, not a morsel of turkey went down his throat despite all offers.

It was a relaxing couple of days. Nana's great hobby was playing cards and if she had turned her mind to it and taken up bridge, she might have gone far, but on these occasions we always played solo whist and she was as successful as she usually was at her other main interest, the backing of horses. Josie and I, and a reluctant Pop, were connived into foursomes which started immediately after breakfast and often went on, save for short breaks, into the early hours of the following morning. We played for small stakes, and the eventual winner (Nana, of course) pocketed a considerable sum.

I got into a bit of trouble when playing as her partner for she was deadly serious and I had the bad habit of playing good hands back to front and occasionally forgetting the rules. When she got to understand my method of play, nothing could stop her. Still, I can recommend cards as a good way of spending Christmas and Boxing Day.

It was late afternoon when two cars drew up outside the house and peering through the curtains we saw a number of familiar figures from Josie's family approaching the front door. There was her Aunt Nance, her brother Roger with his wife Maisie, her sister Joan with her husband Eric, and their three children. It was a Christmas visit with the added purpose of taking Nana and Pop home. We were very pleased to see them and over glasses of wine and lemonade much conversation ensued.

I could only conjecture as to how Maisie would react to Smokey. It was not that she hated cats, rather that she viewed them with abhorrence and fear. It may have been self-inducement but she was sure that a cat's hair that had once landed on her had caused a rash.

She loathed cats - the way they walked, the look in their eyes, their habit of licking - everything. It was an allergy both psychological and physical and one that I found it hard to come to terms with.

Maisie shuddered when she saw him.

We sat down to tea round a large table and had not long commenced when Smokey jumped onto my shoulders. This was quite a normal habit of his but what was unusual was that, not content with surveying the scene, he proceeded to travel from one person to another by walking round the circle of people from shoulder to shoulder.

Maisie was opposite me and she did not appear to notice what was happening until he was actually on her. The children squealed in anticipation, but what happened was unbelievable to the rest of us. Instead of violently starting up and flinging the dreaded creature from her, she remained still, then stroked him as he passed on to the next person.

"Maisie," I said, "I thought - "

"Too true. I can't stand the things but he kind of caressed me and I hadn't the heart to push him off. Besides, he's your pet."

I was about to say all sorts of things but thought better of it. Smokey had returned to my shoulders, purring with contentment. It was his triumph. His love for humans had overcome her innate detestation of his specie and I could only wonder.

Before they left, our pet was being cosseted by Maisie, in the friendliest of fashions, even as she protested that he was the one and only cat she would ever allow on her lap.

Winter soon set in and Mokey had his first experience of snow. When we let him out into the garden he looked at it long and hard before gently placing one paw on it. Satisfied, he essayed a step, sunk in it up to his haunches and scrambled back. I went out to clear a path and he followed me, waiting till I had cleared an area before advancing further.

As soon as he was sure that there was nothing to fear from the white stuff, he ran around the garden with only the top half of his body visible, returned to where I was and rolled over on to his back to have his tummy tickled, wondering why we had not provided this source of enjoyment before. I have never, before or since, seen a cat who enjoyed snow as much.

Unfortunately for him, the snowfall was gone after three days and he was not so keen on the soggy mess that succeeded it.

January passed and we came up to our first anniversary. What had we learned - if anything? Experience had taught us something, surely, for despite our caution we had come upon the house like blind idiots and gone blundering forward with the purchase as if it were a heaven-sent gift.

We had sweated and worked, and scrimped and saved merely so that the house would not crumble before our eyes and if we had not, I think it would have done just that.

There were some plus factors. The second mortgage was already well under way to being paid off and it was unlikely that we would repeat the error of buying an old house without getting it surveyed.

We had discovered that headache of all householders, local rates, and had not been overawed by them. Most important of all - we lived in one of the nicest parts in the whole of the London complex and had got to know some of the local people, if not to any great degree - the café owner, the laundry man, the long serving assistant of Gosling's and so on.

Our newsagent was a man who had a sense of humour. Each week when we paid the bill, he would say, "Who won the race?" referring to our daily sprint to catch the eight-thirteen to town.

We had still had very little to do with our neighbours and although that was understandable on one side, for they had not long moved in and were probably wrestling with their own problems, dry rot and all, it did appear strange that on the other side, where we used to see the woman and not her husband, the situation for several months had been reversed. The man, whom we now saw more frequently, would mutter, "All right," if we enquired after his wife, but we never saw her at all.

He was an old fellow, slim of build and slow of walk and he spoke in a melancholy tone as if the world was too much for him. His wife had once told us that he suffered from migraine and we had accepted this explanation. When, however, we asked him if he still had his headaches, he muttered in reply, "It was her not me."

"I see," I said sympathetically, if a trifle confused. "How is she, then?"

"Not too good. Poorly." Seeing that I was about to press on, he turned toward his back door and a moment later was gone. Very odd. Other enquiries followed from us, but she was always "poorly." Sometimes it was headaches, sometimes her legs were playing her up and sometimes she was "under the weather."

There followed a period when the man could be seen late at night foraging about in the dustbin for minutes before setting light to the contents. This got our imaginations going full speed ahead and the smell from the dustbin accelerated them. Could it be that murder had been committed next door to us? The wildest of thoughts were discussed and we did nothing but wait.

The answer when it came was sickeningly sad and remained a little weird but at least understandable. The old man told us himself for it was patently obvious that he had to unburden himself on someone and we were the only people he had had any contact with.

He said he had led a selfish and lonely life for many years leaving his wife to obtain the food, cook it, do the cleaning and also everything else that there was to be done and he bitterly regretted those wasted years. It was true that he had headaches but blamed it on the indolent life he led, almost that of a recluse. His wife had been a strong, robust woman and had stoically performed her duties for the best part of a quarter of a century, never complaining, never upbraiding, until the previous year when she had fallen ill. She must have been a very strong-willed woman for she resolutely refused to call a doctor in.

She continued to do her best to look after him but gradually got worse and had to be confined to bed. The old man was forced to start doing things for himself and the situation degenerated further when she started bleeding internally and externally from the stomach. He had, perforce, to help her with bandages and cotton wool and it was this that we had seen him burning in the dustbin.

She had gone down hill rapidly but right up to the last would not have a medical man in. On the last day of her life she had consented and in six hours' time had been pronounced dead.

The cause of his wife's demise had been cancer and the old man had then led an even lonelier existence than before, for he had got into the habit of getting his other next door neighbour to purchase food and leave it on his doorstep. Clearly this could not continue indefinitely and recently he had taken to going out again, hence his call on us. We promised to keep in touch and, when he had departed, digested the news that the old woman had been buried without us being aware of it.

Mokey also had a bit of trouble about this time and I thought I knew the cause. I was cleaning and mopping out a room - a small attic, no more than five yards square - when my eye casually alighted on a fly in the middle of the floor. Just as I was about to shoo it off an enormous spider shot out from the skirting board area and seized it.

Shaken by the sight of this awful looking thing, I knew, nevertheless, that it could not be allowed to survive and wander about. A creature that size was surely poisonous though how it got there defied explanation. I took one quick step forward and crushed it with my foot, then fetched a dustbin and brush to sweep it up. Even dead and severely contracted in size, its body was an inch and a half across. Josie refused to give it more than the barest of looks.

Had it been brought in with bananas we had recently purchased or found its way from a hot house at Kew Gardens? Who could say?

The following morning we noticed that Mokey was limping with his back left leg. We looked at him and found there was a large swelling midway between the haunch and the paw, on the inside of the leg. He was very good, allowing us to bathe the affected part with warm salt water, dry it and apply a cream.

"However could he have got that?" Josie enquired.

"Why, the spider, of course. It must have bitten him."

"Maybe it is only a coincidence the two things coming more or less together. There could be some other cause."

"You didn't see the spider alive and full-sized, dear girl. I did." I shuddered. "I would bet that the tarantula, or whatever it was, was responsible."

As Mokey was perfectly all right in himself, a little less frolicsome, maybe, but eating well, we decided to see if it would clear up on its own. So we waited for two days, bathing the affected part in the morning and evening and applying the cream. His limp got no worse but the swelling increased in size to about that of a small hen's egg and looked menacing.

We decided to take him to a vet but that night the swelling burst, emitting a pink, sweet-smelling fluid - a largish quantity - and Mokey lay on his side uttering a full-throated hymn of thanksgiving for his relief. We bathed the place again and when he rolled over for a tickle, we, too, knew the crisis was over and were thankful.

It never ceased to surprise us that Richmond was so rural, for we often came across creatures in our garden that we only expected to see in the true countryside. Apart from the birds, of which there seemed to be hundreds, there were frequently field mice to be seen squirming in the grass, also hedgehogs, the filthiest of animals but delightfully harmless, and squirrels, to mention but a few. One night, though, we saw the creature that never was.

It stood outside the back door, a thing twice the size of a normal hedgehog with long bristles and stumpy brown tail. It was motionless and I called Josie to have a look at it. We could not clearly make out what it was under the moonlight and fetched a torch for a closer inspection. Not wishing to scare it, I tiptoed down the steps and it made no sign that it was aware of my advance. Finally, I leant down and shone the light full on it from a couple of inches distance.

"What is it?" Josie called out.

"An indoor specimen that doesn't usually like the open air, dear. A brush!"

The birds had given us a lot of interest - and now also trouble. During the early summer the fledgling sparrows were dropping down from the eaves, the guttering and the trees at the rate of two or three every day. They nested in their traditional niches at the top of the house, the blackbirds in the trees. The babies who could not fly would squabble, then topple, and once they were on the ground, were an easy prey to any cat that might be in the vicinity, which, fortunately, was not many.

The Moke, as we occasionally called him, would bring one in, in his mouth, drop it on the floor and wait to be congratulated. He never killed them but they were often injured, so presenting a problem. The helpless little things could not be left to perish without some efforts on our part.

We got hold of a small cage, put newspaper, water and a bowl of seed in it, and hoped that the invalids would recover. Josie had read somewhere that if you picked up a bird and applied spittle to the beak, it would get the message that there was nothing to fear, and commence to eat. Sad to say, our efforts nearly always failed.

We also tried hanging the cage with the door open on a high, overhanging branch of next door's tree, with no better success. We kept on trying, though those that did recover made a proportion of no more than one to seven.

Most cats have the instinct to stalk and catch any small thing that moves, and Mokey was no exception, but whereas the rule for felines is to play around for a while with the hapless victim before applying the *coup de grâce*, he never did. Much as we were glad of Mokey's benevolence, it was not a trait that could be positively admired, as it did not measure up to the expectations one had of a cat. It was, in our eyes, slightly unnatural, certainly unusual.

There was one occasion when Mokey brought an injured blackbird in and it escaped and flew off. We thought it had found its way back to the garden but many hours afterward when we lay in bed reading, we noticed that Mokey was looking very intently at a corner of the room. We thought we heard a scraping noise and wondered if mice had invaded, but the search revealed that it was the bird who had survived unnoticed. It was wounded in one of its wings but survived for another two days.

What we did give Mokey full credit for was his ability to answer to familiar sounds; not just conversation but movements. We found this out by accident when, returning home together one day, I fumbled in my pocket for the house keys. We were some way from the house but the instant the keys jangled, he popped his head up from a distance of about ten yards and ran up to us.

After that, it was easy to train him, increasing the distance by stages and making the noise of the keys as loud as possible. Eventually, we had only to turn the corner of the main road into our street, get out the keys and immediately he would appear from the front garden of our house and scamper, with belly close to the ground, to us.

The fact that he picked up the sound of the keys against that of the traffic from about sixty yards away showed he had acute perception.

It may be that doctored cats have their basic instincts diverted - or sublimated - into more refined channels. Be that as it may, it was an undeniable fact that Mokey preferred the company of human beings to that of his own kind.

Sylvester had been no one's friend and the odd cats that turned up in our garden were looked at from a distance by Mokey, with no attempt whatsoever to associate with them in either a friendly or hostile way.

He was territory-conscious only once, when two cats turned up at the same time on the garden wall. He arched his back and advanced, and fortunately they made off.

The preference to be with mankind was not just evinced towards those who fed and sheltered him but to anyone who came into contact with him, notwithstanding that they might be of the tribe that are genuinely allergic to the sight or touch of any feline.

We had been in the house about eighteen months when a small buff envelope fluttered onto the front door mat with 'OHMS' on it.

It was addressed to me and upon opening it I read, 'By virtue of a precept, to me, Sheriff of the County of Surrey, directed, I do hereby summon you to be and appear before Her Majesty's Judges and Justices at the Central Criminal Court in The Old Bailey in the suburbs of the City of London'. It went on to say that I was to 'enquire, present and execute all and singular – ' those things with which I should be 'then and there enjoined'. It ended with these words: 'Whereof, fail not, as you will answer the contrary at your peril'.

What it meant was that I had been called up for Jury service.

I had noticed that there was a 'J' beside my name on the Electoral Roll, but thought it a rare thing to be asked (or directed) after such a short status as a householder. Friends and relations I had known, including Pop, had been on the register all their lives and never been called upon to perform this duty.

I failed not and in due course and with some trepidation presented myself at that place that had been the scene of so many famous trials of murderers and the like. A scene of great activity was apparent both outside and inside the building, but, surprisingly, little sign of security.

The policeman on duty at the entrance gave only a cursory glance at my letter and ushered me in among the hundreds of people milling about, all waiting to be told what they had to do. This continued until an important-looking official came into the hall and called for silence.

Sheets of paper were produced and from them the official read out names and numbers. The allocation to courts took place, by ballot, names being read out in a loud voice followed by the injunction, "Come forward and save your fine of a hundred shillings."

A few people were excused duty on special grounds, including holidays. I was one of the very last to be called and was told to go with some others to Court No. 1. Having arrived there, another long delay ensued, the time being passed with idle conversation, some of the comments being most enlightening.

There was a general grumble about the inconvenience of the proceedings and one man said he would lose business every day he was there. I was fortunate in that the company I worked for had given me leave of absence with full pay for the duration, and all of us would receive out of pocket expenses from the court, which I thought was generous enough - a minority view.

Another gentleman said he hoped he would be put on a case involving a foreigner as the lot of them should be sent back to their own country, or jailed as a nuisance. This was a clear case of prejudice in advance and I hoped he would be disappointed.

Presently the officers of the court came in together with the barristers and their clients. There were two men to be tried and I glanced at them as they were asked if they had objections to make to any of us. They answered in the negative and I wondered what was going through the mind of my neighbour for the two accused were both West Indians. Everybody took their places, the jury of ten men and two women on a raised platform at the side. Silence was called for and we all had to rise to our feet when the Judge entered and bowed. There followed the ceremony of the taking of the oaths. Each member of the jury had to swear separately, by reading from words on a card placed before him, to be fair and just in his deliberations, and after us nearly everybody else connected with the proceedings had to do the same. The Judge was a notable exception.

The two men were accused of using an offensive weapon against a white youth and with carrying an offensive weapon in a public place with intent to use it. They pleaded not guilty and stood sullenly in the dock as the case was put by the prosecution and rejected by the defence.

Witnesses were called by both sides. The youth and his companions had often called the Jamaicans 'dirty niggers' when they had passed them in the street, and on the occasion in question, one of the accused had retaliated with a punch. It was then claimed that the Jamaicans had chased the boys along the street, cornered one of them and hit him about the head with a car chain, thus causing him injury. The youth had been taken to hospital and stitches used for the wound.

Ezra and Jonathan spoke very bad English which did not help their case. They said they had been in England for two years and had come up against racial prejudice many times, not least from the police. They had had great difficulty in finding lodgings and jobs, particularly Ezra who was married with one child. Jonathan was single. Their frustration was understandable but it did not justify taking the law into their own hands.

They had been sitting on a stone wall at the end of their street when the white boys had come along and hurled abuse at them. The youth they were accused of offending against, had stuck out his tongue at them and a minute or so later a stone had been thrown.

They had pursued the boy, Arthur Smith, to find out if it had been he who had thrown the missile and to try to get his address so that they could call round on his parents. All they had done was argue with the youth, but medical evidence was produced to show that the injury had been caused by a chain similar to the one found in Ezra's possession. The laceration scars on the boy's head were still visible and a hospital report said that there had been other wounds at the back of the head.

Arthur was directed to go before the jury so that they could have a good look at his face and head and the car chain was also passed round. Ezra, it was claimed, was the man who had struck the blows as Jonathan had looked on.

The incident had occurred in the Clapham Junction area,

and Arthur was referred to by the immigrants as "one of the Junction boys." He was nineteen, blonde haired and smartly dressed in a grey two-piece, but I was not impressed with the way he gave his evidence for it came out very pat as if it had been rehearsed many times.

The landlady and two other people were called in support of the West Indians, all of whom stated that the accused were of good character. Two policemen gave their version which was that Ezra had been in a very excitable state when arrested, had shouted, "I'll get the white trash next time and do him properly," and had used much abusive language towards the officers.

The police were cross-examined at length and doubt was thrown on the accuracy of their notes. The defence counsel pointed out that to have got down all that was supposed to have been said, with no errors or omissions, would have required a degree and facility of shorthand that they did not possess.

The trial dragged on all through the week, but there were frequent intermissions. The Old Bailey had an excellent cafeteria and it was interesting to observe the lack of formality. Everyone took what they wanted and sat down at the nearest table, thus lawyers, witnesses, jurymen, the accused and general members of the public were inextricably mixed.

It was Thursday before the prosecuting and defence counsels concluded their orations and on the Friday, the Judge, who had been doodling all the week, summed up.

For all his apparent lack of interest in the case, he gave a long and detailed summary, impartially weighing each scrap of evidence in the balance before us. We, the jury, were enjoined to reach a fair, impartial verdict and elect a spokesman to represent us. An officer of the court then led us to a special room so that we could deliberate in comfort and secrecy.

I had often wondered how these things were done and after our walk through the passageways and down the stairs, I found myself and my companions in that room. It was promptly locked behind us by the Bailiff of Jurors, but before he did so, he, too, had to swear an oath that he would not let us out before we reached a verdict.

The room was large with an ample oval-shaped table around which we sat in our twelve chairs. At each end of the room was a door, one marked 'GENTS' and the other 'LADIES'.

On the table, a jug of water and two glasses, a large ashtray, a further small tray for an unknown purpose, notepads and pencils.

Someone enquired if anyone of us had any experience of conducting meetings and when I volunteered the information that I had, I was unanimously elected the foreman.

We deliberated all the afternoon, that is with the exception of one man whose sole contribution to the discussion was "Hurry up and make up your minds about it. I'll go with the majority." I went round the table from left to right finishing with myself and asked each in turn to express his opinion, making notes of what they said on my pad, finally reading them out and asking if they had reached a definite verdict.

The cigarette companies must have done well that afternoon for nearly all of us smoked incessantly and the ashtray was soon full. The floor, also, was littered with fag-ends and ash. By the time tea and biscuits were brought to us at half past four we had decided, but all agreed to have our refreshment before returning to the court.

The verdicts were unanimous, if the one who couldn't care less is included. Ezra was found guilty on both counts, but Jonathan, against whom the evidence was sketchy and circumstantial, not guilty, again on both counts.

One thing surprised me immensely. The gentleman who had been so anti-foreigners before the trial started, was the loudest in his defence of the West Indians. As he put it, "We British are a fair-minded lot and we've got to show these coons what justice is. If it was the other way round and we were in the dock and them in the jury, we'd have been found guilty in five seconds flat."

We knocked on the door and it was opened at once by the Jurors' Bailiff who asked if we had reached a verdict. Receiving the affirmative reply, he conducted us back to the courtroom, which rapidly filled up with an air of expectancy pervading. Such, I should imagine, it is with all cases, no matter how trivial. The Judge, as usual, entered last of all and we had to wait for him to be seated before sitting down ourselves. The time-honoured questions were put to me to answer on behalf of all of us.

If the verdicts were fair and I think they were, the judgement on Ezra was harsh. He was sentenced to a total of eighteen months' imprisonment.

"Take him down!" the Judge ordered and the West Indian curled his lips at him with unspoken contempt. He never looked at us.

So ended the first week and as I walked home from the station, turned the corner into my own street, rattled the keys and waited for Mokey to come bounding up, I wondered what the next had in store.

VI

If that first week was the hors d'oeuvre, the one that followed was a piquant main course. As British justice ground its slow way forward, I, for one - hard-up Theodore - would willingly have forgone the out-of-pocket expenses for the privilege of participating in it.

As it was we were taken around to various courts and sat in on the proceedings, the idea being that we would familiarise ourselves with the routines and rituals. It would have been better if we had done this to begin with, but these visits were interesting and included a complicated jewel robbery case, the essential ingredients of which were who did what and when. The jury had been unable to reach a verdict when they were first sent out and had to have explained to them a large number of legal technicalities before making another attempt.

On Thursday we were given another case for our own deliberations and the charge was rape.

A young Irish girl called Brenda accused a youth of the crime, the defence being that she had consented. In a case like this the evidence can never be verified, it being basically one person's word against another. The girl admitted she was sexually experienced and did not hold strong religious views or have morals of a high order, but speaking in a quiet voice she maintained that she only went with a man if she definitely liked him. Cross-examination did not move her from this avowal.

Her story was that she had left her flat to do her Saturday morning shopping and had bumped into the man, whom she had known by sight. After some conversation, they had agreed to go to her place for a cup of coffee on the strict understanding that there would be no funny business. Once inside her room, however, he had acted like an animal, butting her around, forcing her onto the bed, and raping her. She had shouted for help but no-one had come.

His account was as simple as hers. They had met, she had asked him in, and everything that transpired had been at her instigation. He had merely availed himself of the opportunity she had brazenly presented to him. As it had been broad daylight, his counsel suggested that the noise and shouts had been bound to be heard.

The exhibits, including the girl's undergarments, were passed round for inspection and the Judge gave the precise legal definition of the word 'rape'. A simple case and one could only form an opinion, on the truth or otherwise of the conflicting tales, by the way the two principals spoke and behaved. One glance at the man was crucial and damning. He was well-dressed, but a leering grin on his face looked as if it had been fixed there by years of debauchery.

We were sent back to our room and were out again in half an hour with a guilty verdict. Any lingering doubts we had about our conclusions were swept away by the revelations given before the Judge passed sentence.

The accused had already had two convictions for rape, and a string of other crimes for which he had been found guilty were read out. What was more, he had been brought direct from prison that very day, where he had been already serving a sentence - for rape! Why, I asked myself, had he been let out on parole with such a record? Truly, no matter how hardened the criminal, he gets more than his fair share of justice in British courts.

I wandered around for a while, then caught the tube back to Richmond.

As I had time to spare, I took the opportunity to stroll in the sunshine round some local areas that were new to me and felt I was lucky to be living in such a well favoured outer district of London. That is, if it had been luck that had brought us where we were. When I thought of the strenuous efforts we had made, I thought they had been worthwhile.

Our favourite promenade after Kew Gardens, was by way of the river to the green and there were ways of varying it, sometimes by cutting up the Old Palace Lane or going to the footbridge in The Old Deer Park and so over the river. Spring was the best season with many trees in full blossom of pink and the grass at its greenest.

On this occasion I went over the town's famous old bridge, down Willoughby Road and Ducks' Walk, over Twickenham Bridge and so back along Kew Foot Road. Mokey was waiting as usual.

I put the kettle on and walked out into the garden, Mokey running on ahead. He settled down on our cultivated patch and to my dismay, nibbled at the lettuces. I examined the patch. Every one of the half-grown plants had, in varying degrees, been chewed and the culprit was happily helping himself to more. I muttered to myself, for it's not pleasing to see one's work wasted. So Mokey was not only part cat and part dog, but part rabbit as well.

Remembering what the garden had been like a year before, I was not too displeased with its present state. Of the mass of tall stinging nettles, not one remained, all pulled up by the root, the hardest and best method there was. Couch grass had taken its place but had been kept in some sort of order. Patches of the soil at the end, in the middle and to the sides had been cultivated, and we now had currant bushes, rhubarb, tomatoes, peas and beans besides the lettuces. We had plans to build a concrete path and grow flowers on either side.

In particular, next-door's apple tree was a blessing, and

there was holly to be had in profusion from bushes in the garden that backed onto ours. At the appropriate time of the year, we had seen the owners who had told us we could take all we wanted.

With the cat in front I re-entered the house through the back door into the scullery. From there I went into what was now our kitchen with its tiled concrete floor, modern gas cooker and cupboards in profusion, all surrounded by modern wall paper, three sides being a normal pattern, but the fourth an exotic and refreshing scene of a beach, with the sea in the background.

We had open firegrates in all rooms, supplied with solid fuel from the cellar that ran outwards from the lobby into and beneath the street outside. The manhole that gave access to the cellar, a relic of the days when glowing live fires were the order of the day, still had its use.

Our front room, in which we lived, looked out onto the street and was decorated in the modern style, the furniture being mostly of oak. The walls were plain and provided a good background for the display of the cheap reproductions of famous paintings - self-portraits of van Gogh, Cézanne, Picasso and Modigliani. Not surprisingly, we called our house The Prado.

One thing that our home lacked, and we were determined that within the foreseeable future it would go on lacking it, was a television set. There were reasons not connected with the cost, for we realised only too well what a colossal time-consumer it was. Of those programmes we had been forced to watch when at Nana and Pop's, or at the home of a friend, there were few we would have minded missing, and the drug factor, that dried up conversation, also dulled the senses. It was all stuff going in and none coming out.

It was therefore not altogether surprising that the television was low on our list of priorities as also was the motor-car. Even so, we came to the conclusion that some increase in our amount of locomotion was desirable.

As a boy I had been a keen cyclist and Josie, too, had happy memories of bowling along the countryside in the days before the internal combustion engine had taken over as the dominating factor in transport, particularly in the London commuter belt. We therefore purchased a bicycle apiece and found them extremely useful when popping into the town to do a little shopping, or collecting the laundry, or for any number of other jobs. It was nice, also, to take an occasional jaunt to Kingston, Hampton Court or Virginia Water.

Normally I used my own machine, of course, but there were odd occasions when it was easier and quicker to grab hold of my wife's bicycle and go off on that. Moreover, it had a large carrier pannier on the front into which I could put parcels and bags, and it was on such an occasion - a Saturday morning which was dull with a slight drizzle - that I was cycling along the Kew Road, when I noticed a car coming from the direction of the roundabout.

It did not appear to be going very fast and I thought I had ample time to swing across the road into a side street. I reckoned, however, without two things: the bicycle I was on could neither turn nor go as fast as my own, and the approaching motorist was accelerating. I pushed hard on the pedals but realised I was not getting the desired response in terms of speed that I was used to. Furthermore the car was now considerably closer and instead of turning outwards was veering towards the same kerb as I was.

I could see that the inevitable was going to happen and braced myself for the shock.

There was no mass of thoughts going through my mind, thus proving that it was a myth that the whole of one's life passes through the memory banks of the brain in a few seconds. I had one thought only in my cranium, that I was going to be seriously injured or killed.

At the moment of impact, I took my feet off the pedals and my hands off the handle-bars and sailed off into the air in the direction of Kew Gardens. I stuck out my left elbow which hit the car's side window and smashed it. 'Death is so final,' I thought as the huge wall loomed up. 'Thank God, I didn't go under the car.'

Crash!

The arc I described from the car to the wall was about one hundred and twenty degrees, so I landed at the foot of the wall, feet first, then tipped forward onto my chest, with my head jerking upwards against the brickwork. The main impact was held in check by my hands and arms and fortunately no bones snapped. The car had screeched to a halt.

I was very winded but found I could get up, which I warily did. I could hardly believe that I was not in severe pain and I was truly grateful that I was wearing a heavy raincoat, now heavily ripped and muddy, as were my shirt and trousers. I could see many scratches on my legs and arms.

The driver of the car came up and the old joke about lady drivers came to mind for she was a woman of about thirty and looked very much the dumb blonde type of the middle class. She looked to be in a state of shock as she enquired about me as the noise of an ambulance siren sounded close at hand. It betokened that the accident had not gone unnoticed.

"I'm all right," I said, which was an extraordinary statement for me to make, I thought, and I harboured the suspicion that I had possibly been knocked unconscious without knowing it. Dismissing this thought as nonsense, I declined assistance from the ambulance men despite their persuasions, exchanged names and addresses with the car driver and walked slowly towards Josie's cycle which still lay in the middle of the main road. It had been run right over by the car which was four or five yards ahead of it, yet to judge from its appearance it was not a complete write-off. I picked it up and carried it onto the pavement.

The ambulance man made another appeal that I should at least go in for a twenty-four hour observation, but I thanked him and he went back to his van shaking his head. The accident had happened close to home and mercifully I had suffered no internal injuries that I was aware of, though I was decidedly light-headed when I entered the door of our home - probably some form of shock - which was why I yelled loudly and cheerfully up the stairs.

"Josie - I've had an accident!"

She came running down, took one look at me and exclaimed, "Good grief! What have you been up to? Look at the blood on your head."

"How can I, without a mirror? What's blood, anyway, dear girl?"

"You're bonkers!"

I felt the top of my head and sure enough it was wet and sticky, confirmation being given to me when I looked at my hand. My wife bathed it with warm disinfectant and water, and as she was finishing there came a ring on the door bell. It was a policeman who had called to collect details - that is, my version of the incident - and he enquired whether I was going to take any action in the matter. The thought had never crossed my mind, and having calmed down somewhat, I was still manifestly amazed, and delighted that I was in one piece.

He pointed out to me that I should consider it as I might

be prosecuted by the owner of the car, and if that happened the police would have to examine their report and see if they should take action themselves, against either her or me or both. There was also the question of liability in relation to insurance to be considered.

He was a cheerful constable and when I said I was going to bed to rest, he smiled. "From all accounts, it will be a shorter one than what you nearly had."

When I had undressed I was able to survey myself with the help of Josie, and we came to the conclusion that it was all small cuts and bruises and nothing more. There were masses of them on my arms, legs and chest and a few on my forehead. The only actual cut from which blood had come in any quantity was the one on my scalp and that was not very deep.

I lay down for half an hour but it was nearly lunch time and I was feeling hungry, so got up again and we went off to have a meal. We went to an excellent café at the other end of the town run by Greeks and we stayed there an hour before going off to do some shopping.

It was about four o'clock as we were nearing home that I began to stiffen up and this increased so rapidly that the last few yards to our door became an effort of will to accomplish. Again I undressed and looked at myself. The bruises had come out to an alarming degree on most of my body and particularly on the chest.

There was great difficulty in sitting down and it needed several cushions before I was anything like comfortable. As for lying down and going to sleep, I knew that it would be impossible. It turned out worse than I had anticipated.

I took two aspirins and paced about the room hoping that the movement would relax me enough to lie down, but each time I attempted to do so, the stiffening of the joints and sinews was so marked that it was not possible to do so. It was also barely tolerable to sit up, so that only left me with one choice, standing.

There was a shelf in our bedroom just the right height and by carefully placing small scatter cushions in place, I was able to put my head on them and doze off.

Presently I became aware of something crawling up my back, slowly and carefully and I knew what it was.

When he reached my shoulders, Mokey stretched himself over them with his front paws one way and his back the other. No matter how much I moved and fidgeted he somehow stayed in position the whole night. I could well have done without him as one more irritation, but I was loath to take him off and place him down.

For the next two nights I followed the same routine but took the precaution of leaving Mokey downstairs on his favourite armchair, making sure that the door was shut. I had two days off from work, and did virtually nothing but read newspapers and listen to the radio. By the fourth night the bruises and stiffness had improved enough to enable me to return to my bed, though in a sitting-up stance, and after a further three nights a propped-up pillow at an angle was sufficient for me to get a fair night's rest.

Our gentle cat was allowed back in the bedroom. With his innate sense of what was happening in the scheme of things, the little animal, after spending ten minutes on my bed looking at me with benign admiration, roused himself, jumped onto Josie's bed and slumbered there till dawn.

It was over a month before I was back to what I considered was my normal self and during that period I lapsed into a state of comparative lethargy of both body and mind.

That I had had a near miraculous escape I was sure; but for the grace of God I would no longer have counted as one in the land of the living. As for Josie, she would have been a widow. I had been spared for some reason, I philosophised, and my time had not yet come. If, therefore, my survival was to mean anything, I must continue to act and think positively to the best of my ability.

The immediate practical effect was that I became a more careful cyclist, not that I had ever been a reckless one. Josie's machine was taken to a dealer and the wheels and frame straightened out, the tyres renewed and the handlebars refixed. Such was the avarice of the shopkeeper that he charged considerably more than the bicycle had cost us when new and even had the cheek to add the cost of a new basket that was neither supplied nor requested. In answer to our remonstrances he smiled, waved his arms and said, "The Insurance Company will pay for it. They've got to."

"But it's not insured."

"That's just too bad. You should have done so."

We had a stand-up row about it but we had to pay and that was that.

There were some legal consequences, as the smiling policeman had warned. We obtained a copy of their report which was ambiguous in the extreme, but did give various factors such as the distance the bicycle was found from the kerb, the length of the car's skid marks and the car log details. From this we learned that the vehicle was an almost brand new Oxford and had only clocked up five hundred miles by the day of the accident, so who was to blame?

I came to the conclusion that as with most road accidents it was a case of fifty-fifty responsibility - an error of judgement on both sides coinciding at the same time. So it was left to the insurance company to argue it out in the absence of any police or individual's prosecution.

Letters went back and forth with monotonous regularity until I tired of the whole affair and paid the other side's expenses. Yet I shall never agree that a pedal cycle ridden at moderate speed, hit broadside by a car travelling at approximately thirty miles an hour, could inflict damage to the extent of 'smashed windscreen, smashed nearside window, out of alignment gears, stove-in roof, buckled bumpers, broken driving lights and torn cushions.'

If this was so, how, I ask, could the cyclist, despite his three nights sleeping in the upright, possibly have lived to tell the tale? The answer that might appear complicated at first is very simple. The great insurance game of Great Britain was merely winding its tortuous way through the jungle of finance toward its prey of money, its eyes set firmly on its objective and allowing nothing to stand in its way. The lies and exaggerations that have to be told will be duly recounted but will never appear in the annual balance sheets.

Before, however, the reams of typing paper were placed in their respective files, and others moved down to the archives, human beings prepared once more for the annual jollity known as Christmas. It was our turn to visit and Mokey would have to be a lonesome cat for a few days. Prior to leaving on Christmas Eve, we made special arrangements for him.

A large saucer of boiled fish was placed on the floor of the kitchen, most of which he ate before we went, a second saucer of mincemeat, a third of pilchards in sauce and a dish of a branded cat food from a tin. Two saucers of water and two of milk completed his menus and we hoped he would eat them in the correct order.

This was not so wild a hope as it might appear as we had

noted that if there were more than one saucer put down for him, as occasionally happened, he always commenced with the one on the left. We were confident he would be all right for he still had his cage and his cat run as well as the run of the house. We told him that under no circumstances was he to open the door to strangers.

My parents lived at Brighton and it was almost a year since I had seen them. The journey was an easy one, a leisurely local train to Clapham Junction, transfer via the long alleyway and steps to the platform to pick up the connection from Victoria. For all practical purposes I had broken my ties with my hometown, but in my experience one can never do so completely for it is there that those far off childhood incidents, both good and bad, happy and sad, are etched into the mind. They had seemed so important when they had happened and, as the memory recalled them to mind as we passed familiar places close to our destination, odd emotions stirred.

The streets, the shops, the cafés might have altered somewhat, but were recognisable, but more surprising to me were the faces that stopped before us and enquired how I was. I am not the best of persons when recalling features and I would let the conversation run on in the hope that a clue would emerge as to the person's identity. During the walk from the station, we bumped into a woman pushing a pram with a small child in it and although she stopped us and greeted me effusively, I had not any idea as to who she might be.

We chatted for a while about this and that and it was only as she said farewell that the penny dropped and a whole rush of memories came back to me. Her name was Rita, and she had been a close colleague at my first place of work, in the dark room of a photographic premise. Not many years had elapsed but there she was, married with three children and a fourth on the way. So time carves out a different life for each one of us.

My mother, as usual, had a meal ready for us, and as was the custom in our family, we exchanged presents before we sat down to the meal. There are, for the town dweller, few better ways of spending the festive season than at the seaside, especially with people whose main and commendable object is to let all relax and enjoy themselves, each in his own way.

On Christmas morning, which was bright and clear, my wife and I left the house and went for a brisk walk along the promenade, sniffing the sea breezes, revelling in the exercise, and in my case, happily smiling at places, half-forgotten, half-remembered. It was an ideal way to prepare for the Christmas dinner.

My homecomings did not vary much. There were always relatives, friends and acquaintances calling in to partake of wine and mince pies and to recount stories that had been told many times before, plus a few more recent-ones. If the relish was not always as fresh as one would have liked, it sufficed, nevertheless. Also, there were always at least a few items of up-to-date gossip and the latest developments in the town to discuss and with this kind of endless conversation, it was no wonder that Boxing Day came almost before we were ready for it. Off we went again, promising to write more frequently and stating that we would be happy to see them in Richmond the following summer.

We did not go directly back home but travelled from Victoria by tube to St. Pancras Station, where, after a lengthy wait, we caught the train to Luton, to visit Josie's parents, Nana and Pop.

The journey of barely thirty miles that ensued, must rate as the slowest ever recorded by British Rail, all but three hours in fact. It was slightly misty and the train chugged its weary way forward at about twelve miles an hour, stopping for minutes at every station en route, including a place called Napsbury, which, according to Josie, was the first and only time it had ever done that in her lifetime.

Eventually we arrived and it was almost a pleasure to carry our bags through the streets and along the Moor Park path to the large house where lived Nana, Pop and their feline pets, which had diminished in number to three.

The top cat was Boojems, a large tabby who had been with them five years, and his bosom companion was another tabby named Peter. The third animal was a little Siamese called Shim-Shou who had been given to them only nine months before.

All three had originally been strays and now under the same roof together were friendly enough to take it in turns to wash each other.

Nana was ensconced in a chair with Boojems on her lap, studying the form for Kempton Park, whilst Pop was in the kitchen with Josie's sister, Joan, and brother-in-law, Eric. We spent another two days and nights there, vastly different for there was no seaside front to meander along, and the rule of the house was, as usual, solo - but we enjoyed it. I wondered whether all families were as contented with their lot as mine and Josie's appeared to be, and whether, in the fullness of time we would be the same. It was a somewhat melancholy prospect, not actually unpleasant but standing still had never been my forté.

We caught the early morning train non-stop to town and joined the teeming millions pouring into the underground on their way to a resumption of work in office, factory or shop. The rat-race in full cry! How pleasant it would be if one could acquire means enough to put it all behind one, to contract out having a little more than the bare essentials to live on without worrying, and to be able to do those things in life that were more worthwhile than, for example, pushing a pen and picking up a telephone, on behalf of a company which, no matter how good or bad it might be, was basically soulless.

To be an individual, not a drop-out or a beatnik sponging on the state, but a real person developing the real self. 'Never let your thoughts develop into the state known as a pipe dream,' I told myself. 'Be grateful that you are not living during the thirties when a job, any job, was a blessing to be prized,' and I remembered the tales that had been recounted by my parents about the years that were bad in the true meaning of the word. At any rate it was better to travel hopefully than to arrive, as someone had said, even if one did not think of survival as an aim in itself.

I looked back with a modicum of satisfaction, I had broken away from the suffocating and sterile provincial background, come to London like so many before, achieved a little and maintained a push forward - but I was not content.

VII

The gentlest of gentle cats greeted us on our return with a display of ecstasy. On only one other occasion have I seen an animal of such a proud and independent specie, give such a display of sheer delight at its reunion with its master and mistress - those human creatures who had taken it into their orbit. Dogs go mad with delight, yes, but cats usually prefer to feign indifference.

Nor was it cupboard love. Mokey was plump and had devoured all his food, save for a portion of the tinned turkey. He lay on his back for the hoped-for tickle, purring with a deep-throated roar. He then ran from one to the other of us, brushing himself against our legs and rolling over again. He followed us from room to room and in response to each sentence we addressed to him, he mewed in the peculiar way cats have when excited, as his tail worked overtime.

"Whose bed has he slept on?" Josie enquired and we returned upstairs to inspect. On each bed was a tell-tale hollow, indicating that in all probability he had followed his usual wont by using each in turn. If food had been the test for his favouritism, Josie would have easily won. We stroked and fondled him for some time and gradually the intensity of his pleasure subsided, giving way to placid happiness.

There was post for us both jointly and separately and although we did not then know it, one of the letters was to betoken a most curious happening concerning our pet.

It was from my brother, who had not been at the family reunion. It stated that he was coming to London the following week end and asked us if we would be able to put him up for a couple of nights.

There was no problem about that for our original fold-up beds were still with us, but converted to small tables with little curtains around them and it would be a simple matter to put them back into their function of sleeping apparatus. The mattresses were already inside and we had enough sheets and blankets to make him fairly comfortable though the beds were a little hard. He would surely not object to the temporary inconvenience, although if he did, we could move out of our room and let him have one of our divans. We certainly would not mind doing that.

Timothy was never a man to talk much, so I knew the conversation would be strained to begin with and I knew we would have to force it into channels we were not very interested in. He was tall and gangling and had a secure job in the Midlands, being a carpenter by trade. He had lodged in the metropolis for a longish time before moving north and the tale he told us as the reason for going elsewhere was interesting, if a little out of the normal run of things.

He had been lodging with a couple who had a large family. The husband had been suddenly taken ill with pneumonia and within a short time had died leaving his widow with the task of bringing up six children with ages from one to ten. A month or so after the funeral, the widow had made it obvious that she wanted Timothy to become the head of the household. He liked her well enough but when she had proposed marriage the idea had scared him and he had decided to quit the place. The woman had been several years older than him and the children had looked as though they would be a handful that could not be managed. So Timothy had cut her right out of his life - fair enough, I thought, though I had only heard his side of the story.

Over the years, I had visited Timothy in his London lodgings but had never met the woman or her husband. Whatever the reason, Timothy had always been moody, sometimes given to unexpected bouts of louder than usual laughter and sometimes staring into the distance as if there was something on his mind.

He was a younger brother and I had deduced that he was at a stage of development of the male that urgently needed a mate and found it difficult to find one. So there was little accord between us, but the blood relationship held firm.

He arrived late on a Saturday night on his motor-bike wearing five pullovers on top of his shirt and as he took each one off he emitted a hearty guffaw as if it was the funniest thing in the world. He said the exhibition he had been to had been "not too bad" and would not elaborate on it, though we gather it had something to do with camping which was one of his hobbies. After a quick meal of egg and chips with a mug of tea, he said he was tired and went to bed, happily using the fold-up one we had provided.

Nothing unusual happened during the night and we rose at nine, which was early for us on a Sunday. I took Timothy a cup of tea and biscuits and got on with something else whilst Josie prepared breakfast.

He came down an hour or so later, ate his breakfast, read the newspapers and listened to the radio. We all went out for a short walk returning at eleven. Timothy then announced that he would not be staying. Pressed a little more, he said he had to see someone that evening and when I joked that she would wait, he gave one of his enormous laughs.

After he had gone, we went into the room he had occupied, followed, naturally enough, by the cat. My wife was about to strip the bed when I picked Mokey up, said playfully, "It's a long time since you sampled this one, isn't it?" and went to place him on the counterpane. The result was electric!

From a height of no more than two feet, Mokey

catapulted out of my arms across the room, landing on the floor some yards away.

"What the devil!" I exclaimed, "What's up with you, Mokey?"

The fur of the little animal was standing on end and he was growling as if there was another cat in the room. We were astonished. Gently stroking him, I picked him up again and gingerly approached the bed, but as I was about to place him on it, there was another jerk and the cat was flung across the room again, this time landing on his side.

"He's seen something," Josie said.

"What?"

"I don't know, but whatever it is he doesn't like it."

"This is absurd. How could he see anything? He wasn't even looking that way the second time."

"They do say cats have another sense."

"Maybe."

We waited for a few minutes and once more I went to put him on the bed, for I was not convinced that there was anything untoward with what was only a piece of furniture.

Exactly the same thing happened. It was as if he were hitting a force field surrounding the bed and this had the effect of spinning him off as a ball in a pin-ball machine is spun sharply away when it touches a certain contact. We did not persist any more but sat down discussing the matter. Mokey had certainly been aware of something, but what? Cats do have the 'sixth sense' but what it is and how they react to it is one of the mysteries of life yet to be unravelled.

I remembered an incident that had occurred as a child when my mother's pet cat had given us warning of an unexploded bomb by diving for shelter. That had been explained, if rather unsatisfactorily, as the acute hearing of the animal, who had been able to hear the ticking of the mechanism of the very bomb, from a distance of twenty yards.

In Mokey's case the answer was twice as complex. I satisfied myself that the bed was an inanimate object by lying on it and if there was any psychic force operating, it did not communicate itself to me. It was as normal as a fold-up bed can be. Josie then sat on it holding Mokey in her arms, but he burst free and with fur bristling again went into a corner and stared at the offending object.

Our discussion brought us, as it was bound to, to the one thing that might be a contributory factor to the mystery - Timothy.

He had slept there but his attitude towards Mokey had been normal. He had not kicked him or shouted at him. He had spoken to him, if not in the special tones we used but friendly enough and had given him a couple of strokes. He preferred dogs to cats but like myself came from a home where cats were treated with affection.

The conclusion we came to was, in its way, as bizarre as the episode. It could not be proved or substantiated in any way and in the absence of a spiritualist or an expert on psychic phenomena will have to stand.

It was, we said, Timothy's aura that in part or whole had remained on or around the bed after he had left. The cat had seen or become aware of it and that aura must have contained a strong anti-feline, perhaps anti-human element, completely outside our ken. On the face of it, it was a harsh appraisal, as Timothy, for all his moroseness, had never struck us, up to that time, as a person with a streak so malevolent that it exuded out something that a highly strung cat would react to so weirdly.

The incident passed but was never ever forgotten. Our ménage settled into its familiar pattern.

We had noticed that during a cold or damp spell of weather, Mokey limped a little on the haunch that had, as I supposed, been bitten by the spider. It swelled from time to time as if the joint was arthritic, but such periods were always short and a spell by a hot fire soon cured it. Otherwise, he kept in very good health despite the fleas who persistently burrowed into his thick fur and pestered the life out of him.

Every two months when his licking and biting reached the point when it was obvious the minute creatures were getting the better of him, and he would be sicking up fur from his stomach, Josie would take him on her lap and the tedious job of de-infestation would take place. It might be thought he was a dirty cat, but far from it. He was scrupulously clean in all his habits, but the fleas must have multiplied faster than he could get rid of them, and the liberal application of powder was either of little use, or the pests had got immunised to it.

Fleas were the order of the day about this time. An old friend of mine, William Smith by name, but known as Willie, gave us an unexpected visit. He had not long returned from New Zealand after having lived there and in Australia for four years. He had emigrated under the assisted passage scheme, but the brave new world had not been kind to him. Thus do life's illusions fade.

Nor had the brave old world exactly taken him back to its bosom, for if in Australia he had been a no-hoper, in England he was unemployable. He was not unintelligent but his reactions to ideas and events were painfully slow and people who should have known better, made fun of him. I think he might have been successful in local government.

Whilst doing the round of the employment bureaux and exchanges, he needed a base so that correspondence could be sent to him. Lodgings, however, were hard to find and expensive. We told him he could kip down at our place until he obtained a permanent room or flat. We hoped it would not be long before his problems were sorted out.

He managed to get work with an ice cream company for a few days and took a childish delight in bringing his tricycle to the house and ringing the bell, but his sales were so low that the company told him to go elsewhere.

Then, just when he had obtained a permanent place, he threw it away because he could not get to the office on time.

It was terribly hard to get him up in the morning. "Oh, lore, another day," he would mutter, and then go through his preparations with a painful lack of speed. Meanwhile, we would be frantically dashing around so as not to miss the eight-thirteen. Often we had to leave him in the house and hope that he got out in time and closed the front door behind him.

Nor were his efforts to obtain digs any more rewarding and we were beginning to regret our hospitality. He sank by degrees into a torpid state and did not want to go outside the house. At least it was company for Mokey, who after a little suspicion soon took to him. It was just as well cat-snatchers never visited our district for Mokey would have been easy prey for them. As we used to say, he would have made a lovely fur wrap for someone.

We decided we would find a lodging for Willie ourselves, so we went round all the shop windows that had cards advertising vacancies, and gave him a list of possibilities from which to select. Rather grudgingly he took the list and went out to make his phone calls.

This took all day and part of the next, but by then a landlady had shown him a room that he thought was suitable and moderately priced. The only snag was that he had to go round there again the following day to finalise the matter with a week's rent in advance.

It should not have presented any difficulties for he had the money, but as the time grew near to four o'clock when the appointment was to take place, Willie sat comfortably in an armchair, stroking Mokey who sat beside him. Hints from us having evinced no response, I took the cat away from him, fetched his coat, pushed him towards the front door, opened it and nudged him out.

He stood in our doorway for several minutes, putting on his coat, delaying the dreaded moment, but at last he moved off along the street. Two hours later he was back and proudly told us that he had taken the room and would move out from us within a week.

"There's nothing wrong with Willie," I confided later to my wife, "that a sharp kick in the pants won't put right."

In due course we visited him. He was in a small single room at the top of the house and, as we climbed the stairs, the smell of a dozen dogs permeated the atmosphere. It was a warm evening and as Willie laboriously took the requisite steps to perform the operation known as making a cup of tea, Josie sat down on a chair. There not being another one available, I lay back on the bed that straggled alongside the window.

That night, back at The Prado, I spent restlessly. Waking in the morning, I looked at myself and discovered spots and swellings on various parts of my anatomy. My first thoughts were of chicken pox, for I had read somewhere that blemishes of this sort were the first advents of the disease. I also had a bit of a headache - another symptom - but then I thought of Mokey and his interminable enemies.

Josie confirmed that the spots had indeed been caused by fleas and as Mokey had only recently been gone over with the powder, we decided that the midget monsters had definitely got used to the stuff. It was odd though that Mokey's fleas had never bothered us before, and there had been plenty of them that could have annoyed us. Suddenly I thought of Willie and the dog smell. I rang him up and he quickly confirmed that he also had bites.

"Find yourself another place and in a hurry," I told him. "If a couple of hours' stay can do this for me, what chance have you?"

Banging the telephone down, I dashed up to the bathroom still in my pyjamas. The water was already up to the right point, so without hesitation I got in as I was, and hopefully drowned it or them without further ado. The bed and the bedclothes had to be thoroughly washed and nor was that the end of our so brief visit to our friend.

He had given us an apple apiece and after the fumigating and the application of a lotion, I took a large vicious bite at it, and broke a tooth. For over an hour I thought no more about it, then all hell came to my mouth. A constant, intense pain made life insufferable for both of us.

I was, as they say, nearly round the bend. Aspirins were taken and oil of cloves applied, but the relief they gave was minimal and temporary and I had to repeat the doses. So followed one more sleepless night and although the following morning I managed to fix an appointment with a dentist, it was another full day before he could see me.

He was an extremely kindly and efficient chap and did his best to remove the remains of the offending molar. It would not budge and after upwards of half an hour all he had succeeded in doing was to break it down to the gum.

Finally, apologising profusely and obviously worried, he gave up the task, gave me a note to take into Kingston Hospital, then rang them up and stated that the case was an emergency.

I did not like the sound of that word 'emergency' myself, but being under the influence of cocaine did not worry overmuch, especially as the appointment had been fixed for the following day. Also, I took comfort in the knowledge that the dentist had given me some extra strong pain-killers.

Everything about the hospital was large, modern and hygienic. I went to the out-patients' department, filled in a form and waited with many other people, all obviously in varying stages of pain. When my turn came, I was ushered into the surgery, had my mouth thoroughly examined and was told to return to the room and wait. There I passed a further hour flicking through the pages of magazines and watching the comings and goings.

At last the nurse returned for me and I was conducted to a room that was completely bare except for one chair and a large machine that stood in the centre. It looked like an advanced instrument from outer space technology but was in fact an x-ray machine designed for the specific purpose of photographing the face. Following the instructions of the nurse, I pressed up close to the machine and at the flick of a switch it proceeded to swivel and emit high pitched squeaks, meanwhile taking snapshots of my jaw and surrounding area.

"Call back tomorrow," the nurse informed me when the session was over. "Two p.m. sharp and by then we'll know the results of the x-rays and be able to assess the situation. I think you will have to have penicillin."

The so-called emergency dragged on. By the time I returned I was prepared for almost anything except what actually happened, for after another long wait, this time in another room, the nurse came in to see me and politely but firmly asked me to take my trousers down.

"What!"

"Your trousers. You have to have a penicillin injection."

"I see. I had expected tablets."

I obeyed her although embarrassed (for she was young and pretty), but she plainly was not. A large syringe was inserted into my backside and what felt like half a pint of milk was injected into me. I was thinking, 'All this for a bit of a tooth,' but there was more to come.

"The operation will take place in approximately one hour," the nurse informed me. "In the meantime you should go to the canteen on the first floor and have a cup of tea, but, please, nothing to eat. There's no charge. When you've finished, return to the waiting room and when your name is called it will mean we are ready."

"Thank you."

"I hope you like strong tea."

She actually smiled. So these creatures were human after all. It was a good 'cuppa' that left me wondering if there was anything in it to calm the nerves, though I do not think there was. I did have a nagging doubt as to what was to come, but I had not a trace of toothache and felt wonderfully relaxed, so much so that I was actually looking forward to the continuation and, hopefully, the completion of the whole affair. The only thing I did not want was the return of that awful pain.

There was almost a club-like atmosphere in the canteen as people sipped drinks and chatted with one another. A porter was making the usual mildly flirtatious jokes with the girl behind the counter and a couple of men were discussing the prospects of their favourite horses. I mentioned to them my mother-in-law's keen interest in the subject.

Returning to the waiting-room, I once more waited. When, after what seemed an interminably long time, a nurse, more mature than the earlier girl, entered and called my name, I felt sure that this was to be the final stage in the saga of the tooth. It was a lady dentist and, having adjusted the chair, she looked long and hard into my mouth, compared what she saw with the negatives, and, surprisingly, told me to be brave.

I presume it was cocaine injections I received and during the long operation that followed, my face was turned this way and that, pushed, pulled, stretched and dug at with various instruments.

Then it was over, the offending fragment was out and I was rinsing and spitting in the orthodox way of a person who has had a tooth extraction. The dentist sighed, muttered to her assistant, and then explained everything to me.

"There you are," she said, showing me the object that had been the cause of so much anguish. "The tooth has long roots and they curled round to meet each other in a solid fixture with the fleshy gum intervening between it and the visible tooth. Did you feel anything whilst I was working on it?"

"Not one teeny little twinge," I assured her.

"Good. The nurse will now take you to the recovery room and you must stay there until she gives you permission to go."

"I am very much obliged to you."

"That's quite all right. It's our job."

"Much appreciated."

The recovery room had five other people in it, all women, and they presented a sad picture. A nurse was comforting an elderly lady, wiping her forehead with a handkerchief. She had another hankie held to her cheek. I asked what the trouble was but no-one answered.

The phrase 'recovery room' had not percolated its meaning into me, for my operation had been painless and I was ready to leave, though I expected after-pain. I asked again if I could go but was sternly refused. The groaning lady was taken back to the dentist and I supposed I would have to follow her, but in a few minutes the nurse returned and gave me a bottle of tablets and an instruction list, with the injunction that I was to ring the hospital immediately if there were any complications such as heavy bleeding.

I left the hospital and walked through the grounds to the London Road and along there to Kingston, marvelling at the care and attention I had received from all the hospital staff for the mere taking out of an - admittedly difficult - tooth.

Whatever discomfort I had suffered was nothing to the pain endured following the original fracture of the tooth. I had instructions to eat only soft food for twenty-four hours and this did not preclude ice cream. I sauntered happily along without a care in the world.

Josie was in when I arrived home and Mokey was sitting in front of her gazing up with his enquiring look. She was preparing his food but he came over to greet me with his tail high in the air, as if to say, 'We're all together again.'

"Well?"

"It's out! However, probably I'll be walking about in the middle of the night again. I've been warned to expect it. With any luck it should all clear up now, but - "

"But what?"

"You will never see me round Willie's bug hatch again or eating any of his apples. Be a good girl, will you, and make me a cup of tea, and put plenty of sugar in it."

VIII

There are stages in life for a self-willed individual when stagnation sets in with its accompanying frustration. It should not have happened to us if we had planned further ahead, for we knew we were not the type who were content to go on without a worthwhile object ahead towards which we could strive. Time could have mellowed us enough to produce the state of mind known as contentment, or at least satisfaction, but it had not happened.

It had been hard work and a measure of luck that had enabled us to buy the house, furnish it from its empty beginning, decorate where necessary and make some desirable if individualistic improvements - notably the painting of the front fence in various colours, so that people looked at it oddly when they passed by.

The second mortgage and all hire-purchase agreements had been paid off, and we had the unusual experience of looking around for something to do. There was just the matter of the loan arranged by Mr. Chudwallah, but even this became less of a headache as the months went by and all in all we were financially solvent. In short, we had attained a major objective, that which most folk desire, and were no longer dependent on the whims and caprices of landlords and ladies, be they good, bad or indifferent.

It was nice to go to the theatre as and when we desired, to explore the nooks and crannies of the historic locality and to attend local classes in French and German. To come home, shut the front door and relax in our own independent world of three compatible beings. No one, however, can gain complete independence, even if living on a desert isle, and it is probably not a good thing to so be. In our case, we were far from it.

We were each cogs in one of the wheels of industry, itself a mass of springs and ratchets that interlocked and were forever moving. We wearied of the daily rush to catch the eight-thirteen that sped us towards commerce and administration. The hour-long trip across town, stuck like cattle in a truck known as the underground, began to suffocate in more ways than one. The days of concentrated energy, so that someone somewhere could make a profit or declare a dividend, became more pointless.

What galling memories the system had given me! The epitome was an occasion when a departmental reshuffle had required each and every member to apply for the job he was already doing, now called by a different name. This had so gone against my grain that I had refused to co-operate in it and after a deal of discomfort and hassle had got my way, but what a nasty taste in the mouth it had given me.

It so happened that the company that employed me at this juncture was involved in a triple takeover and, although no one was sacked or made redundant, it was confusing for the employees. Some agreed to move up north, others left of their own accord, whilst the rest carried on as best they could.

In this farcical situation three people in the same office were doing identical work with identical responsibilities. The job that had previously been satisfying and so, up to a point, enjoyable, soured, ambitions faded and all were at the behest of forces many times more powerful than the individual.

The temporary solution for Josie and I was to obtain a local job each, that would get us out of the grind to town and give us a breathing space, but we were too gregarious to want to get away from it completely. Independent or not, we wished to develop in our way, do our own thing, make our own mistakes without harming any of our fellows. Money was not the object, only the means to the end.

Having discussed it for hours, we decided one night that if we had achieved one impossible dream, we could, with an effort, achieve another or at least make the attempt. So was born the idea that although we would work on for the present, in the moderately long-term scheme of things we would purchase a business that would provide us with enough to live on and a little more for the proverbial rainy day.

We knew our burgeoning capital was strictly limited and that we would be taking a very big chance, but the thought urged and spurred us on. It was a far better prospect than security, the syndrome of which held so many in its grasp. Apart from health and strength, so vital in any human endeavour, our one great asset was the edifice that we had sweated and slaved over, that had given us so many heart--searchings and worries, and which, for all that, we were fond of - the house, our home, The Prado.

Sorry would we be to leave it, that crumbling piece of Victorian architecture that we had saved from the ravages of time and neglect, but if it had to be done we would do it. We reasoned that if at the appropriate juncture we sold up and moved into a smaller place, using the experience we had gained to tangible effect, we could do a repeat job far more easily and then find a cheaper place again.

There would be, we hoped, a substantial and honest profit to be made, and this would provide the main capital we would need if our plans were to materialise.

With this in mind, we got down to working on the house once more, cleaning, painting, repairing and generally improving as we thought suitable. Once we had got it to our complete satisfaction, we would keep it so and any small job that cropped up would be accomplished at once. At the requisite moment, the house would be put on the market. Other people had done the same for this reason or that, so, therefore, could we and if we succeeded in finding a buyer at the price we decided, we would be passing a worthwhile house into their care.

The matter was not urgent, rather a need to be fulfilled and we were able to tell ourselves that we were not under anything like the pressure we had been when we had first moved in. As regards experience in purchasing a business, we had to admit that in that field it was nil minus, and the prospect was beset with more hazards by far than our earlier venture. We soon decided that we were thinking too big too soon, or more succinctly, running before we could walk, this despite the resolve to hasten slowly.

The garden gave us a fair amount of trouble. It was not in our ability to turn it into a prize patch but at least we made it presentable.

It soon became clear that if we were to succeed in getting a business, the chances were that we would have to move away from the Richmond area, a matter for great regret, but as we were only in the preliminary stages of our quest, we hoped that when the time came we might be fortunate enough to be able to stay in the area.

On a dummy run, for we were far from ready to take any positive steps, we took a trip to Windsor to look over a newsagents' business. The woman who showed us round had recently been widowed, which seemed a good enough reason for her selling up. We were impressed with the excellent living accommodation and with the garden which ran down to the river, but when she willingly enough showed us the books, we were unable to make out whether they were good or bad.

The object of the exercise was to give us some idea of

what would be involved and in this respect it was successful, though much remained a mystery. The shop itself was somewhat run-down and it was fortunate that at that stage we were not genuinely interested, but it was impossible to say how it would have turned out.

When we were satisfied that we had done all we could in the house, we looked for that smaller property that was to be a stepping stone to the large objective, and after the usual number of abortive attempts, found one that filled the bill. It happened in an odd sort of way.

We had spent the whole of Saturday in fruitless chasing around. Up to Kew, where we were told the house was already under offer, to Barnes where the residence was greatly overpriced, then to another place at Kingston which was visibly crumbling, and two others at Mortlake which were in not much better condition.

All through the day I had been urging Josie to visit a place that was only a bus ride away from where we lived, but she did not like the name of the road and thought the district - Isleworth - was neither one thing or the other, so it was put last on the list.

We were getting a little weary and the evening was advancing toward night. We arrived and after the frustrations of the day expected to be disappointed again. Instead we found a charming little house set in a corner position in a cul-de-sac. The garden, which was surmounted by a tall privet hedge, extended almost completely around the house. We peered over the hedge onto well-kept lawns and cordon fruit trees, besides masses of flowers, and without further hesitation rang the bell.

A woman of about fifty came to the door and, upon hearing our request, smiled and took us in. There she sat us down and explained that she would show us round as her husband was out. She also imparted the information that a couple had only been shown round a few minutes before and they had said they would be back within an hour to give their decision.

At that very moment they would be having a meal, she said, and if they came back they would have priority over us if we decided to make an offer.

The house was in immaculate condition and there was a kitchen which had recently been extended to a size approaching our own, also a greenhouse attached to the back of the house.

I visualised the possibilities for Mokey. A cat flap would be needed for him to enable him to come and go as he pleased and it would be great fun teaching him to use it.

At the back of the garden was a gate leading to the right of way back entrance, which the woman explained was for the use of us and the next door neighbours. On one side of it was a garden shed and on the other a garage, the other end of which fronted the street.

The owner was surely a fanatical gardener, for flowers took up every bit of available space right up the lawn, also the fruit trees and the grass itself had been kept in perfect condition. I realised that if we took the house we would never be able to keep up the splendid appearance. Back in the house we sat in the through lounge and were supplied with tea and biscuits. The woman looked at the clock.

"The hour's up and the couple haven't come back," she said.

"No. They haven't."

"Well, what do you think of it?"

Josie, by now converted, said she liked it.

"Would you like to go for a walk and think about it?"

I considered her suggestion for a while. Time did not have much bearing on the matter but it hardly ever was positively on anyone's side. We had had one of a number of frustrating days that might be followed by many more and I could think of no major objection to the place. It was in good condition, the right size, handy for Richmond, and above all the price was reasonable.

"How much deposit do you require, if we make up our minds now?"

"I don't expect you to have the ten per cent which is the usual thing in these circumstances," she said. "But if you let me have a token amount I can give you a receipt and we can go on from there. You will then have first priority."

I went through my wallet which contained exactly ten pounds and I gave it apologetically to her. She looked at it quizzically for a moment, then made up her mind.

"The banks will be open on Monday, so I'm sure we can wait till the middle of next week for your cheque. One can't however wait forever before deciding. We shall see. A funny thing is we put the house up for sale a month ago but nobody's called until today. It never rains but it pours. You're the sixth lot we've shown over. I suppose it's because we haven't had a board put out, not wanting the neighbours to know we're going just yet."

"Are the neighbours all right?"

"Yes. We're very friendly with them but we'd like to keep it secret a bit longer. Also there's been a case of squatting in the village."

"The village?"

"South Street area. A couple went on holiday and when

they came back found beatniks in their home. Got in through a back window and wouldn't shift. They were kicking up a fuss all night with their radio and record-player, but I believe there's a court order to get them out shortly."

She fetched a writing pad and wrote out a receipt for the ten pounds, and handed it over with the terse comment, "Subject to contract."

"Thank you."

There was a ring on the front door bell and she answered it. The couple who had gone for a meal were back and they wanted to take it. We listened. The woman was apologising to them and stating that she would get in touch with them if the present deal fell through. She returned looking flustered. We shook hands and departed.

"That house, if not cheap, is a bargain," I commented as we strolled back home. "I wonder what the snag is."

"Dry rot, I expect."

"I doubt it." I produced a penknife from my pocket. "I tagged behind you on our tour of the place and in every room I tested the skirting boards and doors with this and they were as solid as rocks. There was no musty smell, no tell-tale cracks, no brown powder. There's nothing wrong with the place structurally at all."

"I hope you are right."

"In any case we will get it surveyed this time, and remember the old saying."

"Which is?"

"It shall be 'subject to contract.'"

No longer first-time greenhorns, we flattered ourselves that our knowledge of house purchasing was as good as anybody's. This was an exaggeration and we had had unexpected pitfalls in the past, particularly in this type of major transaction. Nevertheless, we felt reasonably confident.

"Do you think Mokey will like the place?" Josie enquired.

"I'm sure he will. He will have the time of his life, digging up the rose beds, probably eating the flowers before starting on the raspberries and the pears, and also I noticed a few cats in the back gardens. Perhaps he'll make friends with them."

"I hardly think so. He's not keen on other cats and they're not struck on him. He prefers us and that's a fact."

Even before the weekend was over a snag loomed up. We slept late on Sunday morning and were awakened by a persistent ringing of the front door bell. It was the husband of the lady we had seen the previous day.

When he was sitting comfortably, he stated that his wife, good-intentioned though she was, had no right to accept an offer without first consulting him and certainly not to act as if the deal was cut and dried. Furthermore, she had let it go below the asking price and he was not happy about it.

He was so pompous that we offered to call it off there and then and his manner changed.

"Ten pounds is neither here nor there," I said. "Let's have it back and I'm sorry you've been inconvenienced."

"It's not that I doubt you," he said, "but lots of folk want the place and it turns out they haven't a hell's chance of getting a mortgage. Just dreaming and wasting your time. If you have the money and get the loan, we can discuss it further."

"But you said the price your wife quoted was incorrect."

"Never mind what she said," the man answered, visibly softening. "She did what she thought was best. The price stays but I must make it clear it does not include the garden shed. It's only eighteen months old. You can either buy it as an extra or I'll arrange for it to be taken away when we move. Also the greenhouse heaters, electric cooker and the carpets."

"You take what you feel you want to and we can adjust the price at a later date. I wouldn't expect you to leave the cooker behind anyway."

A long discussion followed and it transpired that his reason for selling the house was that his elderly mother, at present in hospital, could no longer get up the stairs because of arthritis. The way he talked made it appear that there was a long queue of people waiting to buy his house, but we did not contradict.

"There's just one thing," he said as he prepared to go. "I suppose you'll be selling this one."

"Oh, yes."

"Don't let it drag on, will you? Otherwise I may have to go elsewhere. See about the ten per cent as soon as you can. It means you're serious."

I was glad to see the back of him and felt his wife must have a difficult time with him. He appeared to be the sort of person who might raise other points as the sale went on and possibly back out at the last moment, but it was no good acting awkwardly ourselves and until those contracts were signed, we had to work on the assumption that he was in earnest.

When it became clear after a couple of weeks that Mr. and Mrs. Vince were genuine in their desire to sell, we took the next logical step and contacted an Estate Agent about our own place. An estimator came round, measured up the rooms, took copious notes and promised to send us a copy of their house details sheet.

It arrived in two days and they had certainly gone to town about it.

"Just the sort of place I've always wanted," Josie said. "Two minutes to Kew Gardens, though. That's pushing it a bit, and five minutes to the station. Maybe they're hoping Roger Bannister will be interested."

So we waited.

I think it is a curious fact that, at this stage of our lives, having put so much graft into The Prado, and now looking forward to a relatively painless existence, albeit with those long-term plans fixed in our craniums, we started to enjoy those creature comforts that were the norm for most and which we had always disdained.

For example, ever since our marriage we had made do keeping milk fresh by placing the bottles in cold water. We did the same with butter, wrapping it up in greaseproof paper and not worrying that a small amount of water would get inside.

Josie, who had a dislike of gadgetry and liked old-fashioned things, made a token objection but filled up the newly purchased refrigerator with all manner of items.

Our open grate that had cheered us with its live fire, especially when well alight with solid fuel, had an electric fire placed in the hearth. If it was not the same, it was easier to keep clean and gave out ample heat.

Against all our previous resolves, a large black box was placed in a prominent position in our living room and if one pressed a switch and twiddled some knobs, there came forth black and white pictures that flickered and moved, showing images of the entertainment world that had been enjoyed before only in the cinema or theatre.

Mokey did not know what to make of this contraption and would gaze at it in his quizzical fashion. When the picture jumped, as it did every time an aeroplane passed overhead on its way to or from Heathrow, he would go over to it and study it intently until the vibrations faded, when he would return to his former place.

After a few days, he decided it was a rival to his part in the scheme of things in our cosy little world, jumped on top of it and sat there looking at us with his tail gently swaying from side to side.

As for us we started off by watching the news only, but soon progressed to sport, documentaries and plays, and if we did not become addicts in the accepted sense, we nevertheless did our fair share of watching the goggle-box. At least it took our mind off the wearisome business of house buying and selling which turned out to be every bit as long-winded as we had feared.

There was a lot going on in Richmond at the time, including a much publicised pop concert and this showed us in stark relief how at least a portion of humanity regarded the world it inhabited.

It took place in the Old Show Grounds and the music, blaring incessantly in the ears of those who lived within a mile's radius, kept the townsfolk awake until the early hours and beyond.

The real spectacle was in the streets of the little town. The parade of the great unwashed. They were there in their thousands, roaming round the streets on Sunday, with long unkempt hair, glassy eyes, sallow cheeks, tangled beards and tide-marked necks, their bodies covered in multi-coloured rags that polluted the fresh Surrey air. Was it necessary to so cock a snook at society by providing a spectacle of what they hoped would replace the present set-up? If so, it would convince few.

In a way I pitied them for they had lost their way in the concrete jungle and were not capable of seeking a good way out or of adapting themselves to the environment whilst retaining human dignity. They could only sink into the foliage and revert to the animal level. Not all were like that. I condemn too harshly, but it was the dirty and smelly ones that provocatively drew attention to themselves.

Rebels without causes never make sense. The crux of the problem was to find them a worthy channel, that would enable them collectively and individually to go forward solving problems without inflicting their slimy habits on the rest of society. It did not mean that one should accept things as they were, for no progress is ever made without struggle, and progress itself can be questioned, but the drop-outs only down graded themselves in the general melee.

IX

For some years it had been our habit to go to bed very late and this was deliberate, putting into practice the theory that if we were really tired we would sleep better than if we had merely got into the routine of the clock. We have argued the point with insomniacs who went to bed at ten p.m., took pills and wondered why they did not work, as they tossed and turned and woke up bleary-eyed.

Nana was a case in point for if she could not have a lengthy period of card-playing she would retire to her room, take her drugs, read a book and hope that she would sleep. That she did not, we often told her, was because the nervous and physical energy that should have been released during the day was bottled up in her, so that she went to bed when she was wide awake.

I had urged her to take up charitable work or take a part-time job that would consume her energy. I also reasoned that life was short enough as it was without spending a greater period than was necessary in a comatose state.

The clock could not be discounted as the arbiter of events, that we agreed, but the rule in our ménage was 'never go to bed before midnight'. On those rare occasions when we could not find occupation for ourselves before the witching hour, and there was nothing interesting on the box, we would read or fiddle around with something - anything - glancing at the clock repeatedly, or wait for the time signal on the radio, and then commence the undressing sequence.

Generally, the system worked for us, but getting up in the morning was a problem for we slept deeply and had to rely implicitly on the repeater alarm clock to rouse us from our slumbers. This instrument had been a good friend to us for a long time but like all mechanical contrivances could not be expected to outlast the strength of its parts, so it began to falter and let us down. We persevered for a while, but it became obvious that it would have to be honourably retired and replaced.

On the third morning when it was supposed to go off at seven o'clock and repeat its urgent clangour a minimum of five times, it stopped completely, but I was woken up on the hour by a curious sensation.

A closed eyelid was opened and my eye looked into the little face of Mokey, who was standing with one front paw on my chest whilst with the other, talon extended, he had levered up the eyelid. Once he saw I was awake he withdrew the paw and waited for my reaction.

At first I was amazed, then annoyed. I roused myself and was about to push him away for doing this stupid thing when I caught sight of his look of happiness and stroked him instead, and he purred. As I got out of bed he jumped off and stood on the floor looking at me with his tail high and beatitude on his countenance. How could I take umbrage with him?

I pondered the matter, realising full well that a slip on his part or a sudden movement of mine could create a dangerous accident, possibly an injury to the eye or a nasty scratch on the cheek. He had pulled the eyelid back so gently, however, that I had barely moved and I conjectured that it must have been several minutes before he had managed to wake me. He had obviously meant well and if I wanted to stop him repeating the action I would have to make sure that not only did he not sleep on the bed in future but not in the room itself. Unthinkable!

My wife did not believe me when I told her. She said I had made it up for some odd reason, or dreamed it, and we had a little argument about it.

"He will sleep on your bed tonight," I said irritably, "so be prepared."

"I don't think I'd like to be woken that way. He might make a mistake and I'd find I'd only got one eye."

"Put him in the kitchen, then."

"What for? You imagined it."

Mokey was not exiled to the kitchen, that night or any other night, and the following morning repeated his performance, but this time for my wife's benefit. She had to believe it then and was most concerned for she genuinely believed, as I did, that to be woken by a cat in this way was a chancy business, no matter how gentle he was. Such, however, was our affection for Mokey, that we did nothing about it except to get that new alarm clock, set it five minutes earlier than normal, and mentally tell ourselves to wake up placidly.

Mokey repeatedly woke one of us after that in the same fashion and if the alarm beat him to it he was probably a wee bit disappointed. We never once came to any harm and I was able to see a demonstration of his act when I awoke early one morning and saw him do the whole thing.

Rousing himself from his curled up posture, he solemnly went through the cat's ritual of stretching himself, washing and scratching. His ablutions completed, he looked upwards to Josie's head, stood up and ever so slowly advanced forward to her shoulder. Next he placed a paw on her forehead, and satisfied as to his touch, removed it and gently put it on her closed eye. As nothing happened at this point, he lowered it little by little, pushed again and extended a talon underneath the lid. The eyelid flicked upward and she was awake. Satisfied that his task was completed, he waited for his reward which was a grateful stroke of his forehead.

Then there was the cuckoo-clock, or more strictly speaking, for it had no bird, the Black Forest clock, that we had purchased on a whim of Josie's.

This instrument had a dial surround in dark wood engraved with figurines behind which was the primitive mechanism. A pendulum was suspended from a small hook and on either side there were chains, which had to be pulled to wind the clock up. This we regularly did before going to bed each night and the instrument kept good enough time, gaining only about a minute a day.

Mokey was fascinated by it and soon got into the habit of pulling a chain himself, just once or twice, now and then, and then he would sit back on his haunches and watch the pendulum swinging to and fro. Of course, this gave us great amusement, and the first question we would say to him when we came in each evening was, "Have you wound the clock up, Mokey?" He would slowly wag his tail and gaze first at the clock and then at us - pleasure personified.

What a funny little creature he was! I could not but contrast this little animal's so gentle actions with that of a girl who worked in the same office as myself.

I had left my job in town a few weeks before and Josie had gone over to temporary work so the mad daily rush for the eight-thirteen no longer occurred. The position I had obtained was in the service department of a large commercial organisation and the work I did was simple, namely to answer customers' complaints over the telephone or by letter. It took little out of me. Still, although the salary was less, there were no fares to pay and the saving in time was roughly twelve hours a week.

It was a large office occupied by ten women and four men and the practice, as with most offices, was that when anyone had a birthday, he or she would buy cakes for the rest of the staff. I had a positive dislike of eating between meals, except when on holiday, and when these occasions occurred, I would politely decline, at the same time assuring the person concerned that I wished them a happy day, which, of course, I did. It had always been accepted that it was an idiosyncrasy on my part, or that I was dieting.

On that particular afternoon, the girl in question, a pretty lass of twenty-five, was extremely annoyed and I was about to suggest that I take the cake home, when she acted, (I was going to say like a cat but that would be most unfair) like a wild animal. She sprang at me and with long red fingernails tore two great scratches on my left cheek.

It would be an understatement to say I was taken aback, but certainly I was bewildered, horrified and the object of great sympathy from everyone. It was explained to me that the girl - whose name by great coincidence was Josie - was going through a difficult period in her home life and had reacted violently before to minor incidents.

She swiftly apologised saying she did not know what had come over her to cause the unpremeditated action and I went off to bathe my cheek. Later, when we had got to know each other better, we became good workmates and as regards the cake-giving ceremonies, I would take the article and place it in my desk drawer.

Like all cats, Mokey loved to explore. When the grass was long he would make his way purposefully through it, stopping now and then to observe with interest a crawling ant, or a bee on the clover, and he once found a tortoise that had strayed into our garden. We picked the creature up as it plodded its way forward and discovered that it had its name and address written on sticking plaster on its back, so were able to return it.

On just one occasion our normally cautious pet got

overconfident. He climbed next door's apple tree further than he should and we found him mewing for help. We fetched a long ladder and I made a perilous ascent. I had expected him to panic but his confidence in me was more than I had in myself. He consented to be picked up with an outstretched hand and placed round my shoulders whilst I slowly came down again.

"Cancel the order for the fire brigade," I said with mock bravado and a face popped up from over the fence. It was Mrs. Bonney, the next door neighbour.

"That was a silly thing to do," she said. "You could have broken a leg."

"True," I answered. "And so could he."

Her look of complete disbelief made me feel that I was an absolute idiot.

The following weekend two hefty young men arrived next door and, armed with ladders and electric saws, climbed the tree and cut off the top branches, making such a good job of it that we were able to gather enough fruit from our own garden to satisfy my hunger for apple pies for months to come.

When we had first arrived in Richmond it had been in the nature of a great discovery. We had known so little about the historical connotations of the town and surrounds, but by now they had sunk deep into our consciousnesses.

What was more surprising was that we had strong personal ties that we had forgotten. It all came to light with conversations with Nana and Pop and, from my side, letters from my mother.

Josie's parents had worked in service at Richmond hotels in their younger days and knew all the nooks and crannies of interest. My mother had been born and bred in neighbouring

Chiswick, and in her childhood had spent many a happy day on the towpath or in the gardens. I was reminded by her that I had relatives at Isleworth and Twickenham and old friends still living in the district.

So we had unwittingly returned to family backgrounds and were urged to renew some at least of those long-lost associations.

It was with some reluctance, that, accompanied by my parents, we made a visit, for I had the awful feeling that we would have nothing in common and would have to sit restlessly for two or three hours, making polite conversation and feeling anxious to get away.

Even with my mother and father, I would feel, after a few days of intrinsic companionship, that the association was wearing a little thin, for the truth was that our interests had diverged enormously from theirs and the point would be inevitably reached when we began to bore each other. Fortunately their visits lasted under a week so that breaking point was never reached.

We did our best to entertain them, probably too much, for they were content to talk and reminisce, and took only a passing interest in the sights of the district. Our one great success was when we took them to London Airport and my father, at least, could have remained for hours watching the arrival and departure of the planes.

When he was first taken on a tour of The Prado, my Father could hardly believe that we had accomplished all those little jobs without outside help, and I had to explain that necessity, that is lack of cash, was the spur that had driven us. I showed him a ceiling that had once had a large hole in it that we had thought was too difficult for us to repair. We had had to fetch in a jobbing builder, who had started the work, then left it, so that I, perforce, had had to plaster it up myself, slowly and painfully, but it was accomplished with success.

The visit to my aunt was, for my parents, a must, and it turned out better than I had expected. She was a very game and intelligent old bird - and well up with the contemporary scene - and we agreed to keep up the renewed association.

Human relationships - that was what life was mainly about: the cement that held the structure together; and Nana and Pop were a good example of this.

They were, to use a phrase that is often viewed contemptuously these days, of the old school. That is, they had lived and striven through two world wars, had brought up a family of five, had known what real poverty was, as opposed to the modern synthetic type, had worked a five and a half day week with one week's holiday a year and had preserved their integrity and cheerfulness. Pop was fond of telling the tale of how he had once walked fifteen miles for a job because he could not afford the fare, and how overjoyed he had been to get it. That, for him, was real attainment, and who would deny it?

From the roots of poverty, he had slowly and painfully carved out a better life for his wife, family and himself, and now, not far off retirement, was happy to describe his circumstances as "comfortable".

They owned a large house that had been converted into a hotel and many actors and actresses who later became household names through the medium of television had spent a week under their roof. Extremely good-hearted, Pop had never been known to refuse help to anyone and had a rough and ready vocabulary that disdained accent.

We had been too independent to approach him at any stage of our financial struggles but if we had, for instance, asked for the loan of a hundred pounds, his probable answer would have been: 'Bloody hell. A hundred quid! When do you want it?'

I had grown as attached to him as to his daughter. Nana had taken longer to get to know and appreciate, and I had hadto overcome the mother-in-law syndrome. We had often stayed for a weekend under her roof and she had wanted things arranged for Josie the way they always had been. That had led to a certain amount of friction, but over time, things had been happily resolved. If we did not always see eye to eye, at least each other's point of view was tolerated.

As for the two of them, they often bickered and argued about their past, and as for their tears and travails over the years, they could say with quiet satisfaction that the children loved and respected them, looked up to them for guidance and indeed often took over the house from them. It was a happy family.

As I took their bags on a Christmas Eve, I reflected not only on the past, the finer details of which were theirs' alone, but also on the future. For if time was, as ever, changing, the basic factors of human existence were immutable. A man was born, struggled, had ambitions, failed, succeeded. A man died. It needed a very philosophic philosopher to be able to come to terms with his lot if he had started out with a driving force that brooked no obstacles.

Yet, I reasoned, if Nana and Pop had once walked those Richmond streets, explored those alleys, gone over that bridge, they may well have thought and planned and hoped as we now did. Life had finally settled the matter for them and would do the same for us.

As things stood we eagerly awaited the new year that promised much; a new home and possibly a new business venture which would tax our energies but fulfil a part of ourselves, that long desired satisfaction to be gained by working for just us.

Before that, in the very near future, a holiday that might be our last for a considerable time. Skiing in Austria promised to be unusual and exciting and we were determined to make the most of it.

As we ate the food, drank the drinks, cracked the nuts, pulled the crackers and played those interminable card games, the world seemed a very good place to live in.

It was late on Boxing Day when, as we walked to the station, a light snow was falling and it was very cold. We were glad to get back to our nest and after a quiet drink on our own got on with the task of clearing up the debris. The Christmas hangover as the result of too much to eat, too much to drink and not enough sleep, crept over us, but we consoled ourselves with the thought that another day of the holiday remained.

It was just as well for a glance out of the window revealed that it was snowing heavily. I wondered if any of the pipes would burst, for the house was very prone to this and at the first sign of cold weather, I would place small oil lamps around the areas that we knew would be most affected, but they were not always efficacious. This had not been done as yet. A quick inspection of the vital points, including the loft, assured me that we were not too late to take the precautions, but the sight that met me when I opened the back door was not reassuring. Already the snow lay heavy on the ground and was being piled up against the wall by a fierce wind.

We kept a watch on it. In a matter of hours the blizzard had covered the garden in a deep carpet of white and the snow had piled up as high as the windows, obliterating the cat-run and wall from view.

The sound of shovelling could be heard next morning and

although we had half expected it, the depth of the fall was uncommonly bad. With an effort I pushed open the front door and was amazed, for it seemed impossible that the enormous quantity of snow everywhere could have fallen in one night. All the way along the street, cars stood covered in the stuff to a depth of several inches and the owners were busy sweeping it off, whilst other folk dug their front paths, piling the snow in the roadway.

Soon I joined them, confident that the conditions would not last more than a day or so, for it was generally acknowledged that, whatever else happened in the rest of the country, the London area got off lightly, but in this assumption we were wrong.

It snowed on and off all day, only giving a reasonable break in the evening. We took the opportunity to go for a walk and take photographs of the sights, a chance that might not come again for a few years. So, clad in Wellingtons and many warm clothes, we took pictures of the local landmarks including the pagoda and the bridge. There was little traffic in the town and everyone seemed taken by surprise.

The main roads were being belatedly salted and gritted but no buses were running and few shops were open. We were lucky enough to have a good stock of fuel in and, when we returned with cold feet, it was nice to see the glowing fire through the closed curtains. Once inside it was easy to say that there was no such thing as bad weather.

However, when we returned to work the following day the outlook had not improved and although it had stopped snowing, the louring clouds promised that there was more to come. I was not surprised to find that over half of my colleagues at work had failed to beat the conditions and arrive, for the transport was chaotic. 'The worst snowfall this century', as it was described in the press, had almost brought the country to a standstill and for once in a way the south-east had suffered the worst. A complete state of unpreparedness prevailed, resulting in slippery roads, iced up rail points, signal failures and frustration on all sides.

The milk we picked up from the doorstep was frozen solid and had pushed the bottle tops upwards on little cylinders of ice, our overflow pipes had huge icicles hanging from them down to the ground where they formed a solid base against the side of the wall and some of the water was forced back into the house.

For the first time for ages I had to get out the blowlamp, climb the ladder to the loft and with the aid of a torch, play the heat on the joints of the main water tank which, to judge from the thin layer of ice on the top of the water, would freeze-up during the night.

I developed a cold and began to have doubts about the wisdom of our holiday booking, for if England was like this, what kind of conditions would be prevailing on the continent? With Pop remaining at Luton, this time we had arranged for Nana to house-sit for us on her own. How would she manage if the pipes froze? She could hardly be expected to go around in the dark with a blowlamp.

The New Year's Eve was spent huddled round the fire and, before Big Ben rang out heralding the end of the old and the beginning of the new, we watched the intrepid revelling of those souls who dared to brave the icy water in Trafalgar Square, cavorting about as if it were Spring.

I am usually confident about the prospects for a new year, but as 1962 was replaced by 1963 I did not feel the ebullience rising up inside. With such weather it was hard to think of daffodils and tulips, cricket on the green, birds hatching their chicks and all those signs that the good earth would return to normal.

As days passed and the arctic conditions tightened their

grip, freeze-ups at the house became an all too familiar event. The blowlamp became the daily tool that kept the ice at bay both inside and out. I got into the routine of climbing up to the bathroom last thing at night and from there to the loft, heating suspect pipes and weak points that had given trouble before.

Things eased in the streets as the authorities tackled the problems and the trains were running, if not on time, whilst the buses took the extra load. The queues got longer and the passengers more irritable, but progress was maintained.

The thought of cancelling our holiday recurred every day, as did the hope of a thaw, but nothing was decided about anything. If the temperature went up a little so did our hopes, but if it went down again our gloom went with it.

As usual the issue was decided for us. Nana arrived on the day before our departure and pronounced herself fully fit for whatever rigours might lie ahead. We took her around the house pointing out where she might expect trouble, but her main concern was for us. It was not a very propitious way to embark on our trip, and in my heart I was looking forward to the return - not the best frame of mind in which to go forth and enjoy a holiday.

As for Mokey, the weather had got at him, too. The novelty of the snow had worn off. He was not able to go out much and his thick fur only mitigated the coldness, so he spent long hours gazing into the fire. When the bags were packed and on the floor he knew we were going, and on the night before we went slept on an armchair as if he knew that would be his place for the next week.

As was expected, we went to bed very late, Nana insisting on staying up to watch 'That Was The Week That Was', and it was the clang of the alarm that roused us. Last minute instructions were given to Nana and then it was goodbye to her and Mokey and we were on our way.

"We might as well have stayed in England and gone to Box Hill," I feebly joked, and it was a fact that people had been skiing in Surrey. As if to emphasise the point, I slipped as we reached the station.

The arrangements were somewhat unusual. We were to fly out and return by train. It was the first time we had travelled by plane and I began to wonder if it would not have been quicker overland. First we caught the tube to West Kensington and from there made our way to the reception centre, where a long wait ensued. Then after some formalities a coach took us through the streets and past the white-clad fields to Gatwick where a further long delay followed.

In all it took us five hours from our home to the moment of departure and it was not only the weather that was to blame.

It was an old-fashioned, frail-looking craft with pieces of wire straggling from the fuselage, and it did not look particularly safe standing on the tarmac. Also we had heard that charter flights did not have such a good record as those on schedules, but it was no good being dubious about it.

It was a novel experience for us, boarding, taxiing across the tarmac, the revving of the engines, fixing of the safety belts, and being lifted with a rush high up into the sky. By contrast, the flight was boring.

Whether we looked up or down all we could see was white, relieved for a short while by the Channel and odd bits of greyish-brown, presumably towns and villages. We whiled away the journey with a snack meal served by the stewardess and a game of pocket chess. Although the journey took not much more than three hours, it seemed a good deal longer.

The best part and the most spectacular was passing over the Alps, rugged and menacing, and a few minutes later pine trees were rushing up to meet us as the plane made its landing approach. There was a slight jolt and we were roaring to a stop on the airfield, an infinitely smaller airport than Gatwick and, at present, bathed in bright sunshine.

The first thing we noticed in the reception lounge was a man being carried out to the tarmac on a stretcher and we were told he had broken a leg the previous day. There were about a dozen of us in the lounge and a girl of twenty-five, dressed smartly in a claret and pink uniform, came up and introduced herself as Maureen, the Courier. Soon after we were whisked away to a small shop in the town of Innsbruck to be kitted out.

The place was very much geared up for winter sports. There were a number of places advertising skis, anoraks and other necessities, and that the season was in full swing could be gauged from the number of skis stuck into the snow, left there, doubtless, whilst their owners went for refreshment in the cafés of which there were plenty.

Then we were taken to a guest house that was to be our home for a week - The Hechenmoos, which meant, I thought, hedge moss - a large wooden structure that fitted into the setting of hills, trees and snow admirably. It was early afternoon and a meal was waiting for us.

As we sat silently eating a meat salad with bread and butter, our attention was drawn to some of the guests who had arrived before us and who were now coming down the wooden staircase in the corner of the dining room. They descended slowly, a man on crutches, another with his arm in a sling and a woman with a heavily bandaged head, and others that followed did not appear to be in good shape. The conversation round the table flowed more freely. It is amazing how other peoples' misfortunes brighten everyone up. It was, however, a sobering introduction to the art of skiing.

The guest house lounge had parquet flooring with a large open fireplace at one end, and, rather incongruously, a Juke Box at the other which was blaring out in German an English pop tune. The tables were grouped in the middle of the room and the walls were decorated with Alpine murals.

Our room was on the first floor and was very warm compared to our own house but the air was dry due to the central heating. When we looked out of the double-glazed windows we saw a very pretty picture postcard scene, a little overdone if anything for some of the outside walls of the buildings had pictures painted on them.

The furniture was adequate and included a large box that was also a cupboard which contained blankets and shelves. Besides sheets, the beds had on them large thick duvets.

We unpacked and walked from the village, about a mile to Innsbruck and surveyed the shops. A large thermometer in one window registered the temperature as fifteen below zero Centigrade, but it did not strike us as cold as in England, for the atmosphere was not damp and it was pleasant to be out in those brisk conditions. What made things so vastly different was the panorama of hills and mountains that stretched away into the distance.

We decided to take a short cut back to the village and, not surprisingly, got lost. It was a chance for me to try out my German and we were soon directed back to the main road where we were fortunate in being able to catch a bus back to the village. It was packed to capacity and I counted no fewer than twenty-three standing. London Transport would have had a heart attack.

The juke box was going strong as we entered The Hechenmoos. A party of schoolboys with two masters had arrived from Rugby and quickly thrown off their English reserve. What their parents would have thought was another matter. The lads were aged around the fifteen year mark and some were lounging about smoking cigarettes and drinking lager. They seemed to be well off for spending money and I noticed one boy treat his master to a pint of the beer. The other adults did not appear to be so happy.

At breakfast, the following morning, some people were disgusted with the usual continental repast and went off in search of the traditional English breakfast of eggs, bacon, toast and marmalade, so missing the first session of ski lessons.

We approached them with trepidation but the young Austrian instructor was the personification of patience and much to our surprise we soon learned how to turn, climb and, most important, how to stop. True we suffered some falls but at that rate of progress had visions of doing a downhill run very quickly, just like they did on the television. We enjoyed the day immensely but were glad when it had finished for the unexpected exercise of muscles long neglected soon began to take effect.

The English schoolboys made whoopee in the evening, plying some locals with liquor and making fun of German food and customs, all accepted amicably, perhaps not understood, as the masters tolerantly sat back and watched them.

Josie was in a strangely quiet mood and reclined in a chair reading books all evening, and an elderly local German remarked to me, "Frau, immer lesen." I was slow to get the sense of it but once having done so could follow the rest of his comments without much difficulty. The Austrian-German has a much softer dialect than pure Deutsch with a trace of what we would call a country drawl.

Everybody had stiffened up after their exertions and to judge from the remarks there would be a few absentees from the slopes on the morrow.

Spying an English newspaper I eagerly grabbed it. It was the previous day's and in the north of England it was snowing again. How was Nana getting on and had there been any burst pipes?

These were the questions that came to my mind, and they returned repeatedly even during the following evening which was the occasion of a delightful Tyrolean exhibition of the Austrian Schuhplattler dancing. Apart from those brooding thoughts, it was a pleasant if strenuous time spent mostly in the guest house about a mile from Innsbruck, or on the slopes, alternately skiing and falling.

We sampled the delights of Austrian patisserie, so superior to the British variety, and surprisingly cheap, and consumed plenty of the local drinks of lager and Apfelsaft. The little chalet-cafés on the mountains were reached by chair lifts and once the summit was reached, there were superb panoramic views to be enjoyed of the villages, with glorious backcloth scenery of the mountains. Our skiing, too, improved by leaps and bounds.

Probably the most engaging character we met at The Hechenmoos was the old German who had remarked on Josie's reading habit. He would seize on us as soon as we entered in the evening and gabble away in dialectical German, whether we were prepared to listen or not. We christened him Hitler, because of his moustache, wisp of hair across the forehead, and the violent way he threw his arms about, but it was hard to imagine that the ex-Führer, grown old, would take refuge in this so relaxing little village inn. At least, this gangling and voluble Alte-Herr amused us and we encouraged him with drinks and cigarettes to unburden himself.

One evening he had had a little too much and we gathered from the angry shouts of the hostess that he had better shut up or get out. He subsided immediately and we felt guilty about it.

The Rugby schoolboys went back home and the air of frivolity subsided. There would be another party arriving from England but we would be gone by then and the rest of the holiday was somewhat anti-climactic. Even so, there were compensations for we were able to receive individual instruction on the slopes and were able to take a ride through the countryside on a horse-drawn sledge.

The driver was bitter about the British who had killed his son during the war and lost him a leg. He could speak English reasonably well and we had a long conversation with him, pointing out that whatever side one was on war was futile in itself. "Yes," he said, "It must never happen again," and we parted good friends. I cherished the hope that we had given him food for thought that might one day ease his memories.

Most Germans we met were the opposite to the sleigh driver, going out of their way to be friendly and plying us with drinks that we did not always wish to accept. Sometimes their eagerness to forgive and forget was decidedly embarrassing.

Two little English boys on the slopes excited a lot of interest and would have different tales to tell their friends when they went home. They were tiny tots of four and five years of age. To the great delight of his parents, one cherub proceeded to ski like a veteran after barely an hour's instruction and put the rest of us to shame. Not so the other who hated the whole business and, yelling that he wanted to go home, was sadly led away by his dad.

So the days went, each one different in its own way and

the occasional English newspaper we got hold of informed us that there was still snow in England too. It was hard to believe, as hard as it was to accept that we were soon to go home and without a scratch between us. We were able to ski entirely on our own from the top of the surrounding hill back to the front door of the Hechenmoos, besides being able to do figures of eight, slalom and pull up as and when required.

It was the 'mechanical contrivances' that gave us most bother. There was one drag lift that pulled us up a steep incline at such a speed that Josie said her heart had shifted from its correct position and I felt, too, that parts of the body were being swirled about.

We were congratulating ourselves on the last day that we had come through all the rigours safe and sound when the snow and ice gained a belated revenge and put us firmly back in our place as amateurs.

First we were both thrown violently off of the drag lift during the final skiing session through the sheer stupidity of a girl who announced with a shout that she was "going" and promptly let go, throwing everyone else off in different directions.

Having got over that, I became over confident in my ability to pull up in a second, went straight into a tree and received a black eye, bump on the forehead and bruised lips. That should have been warning enough but Josie was not to be outdone, and falling heavily, twisted an ankle, receiving lots of attention in so doing.

The instructor was a pleasant young fellow called Helmut and he promptly fetched a stretcher-sledge, lifted her gently onto it, and, to the cheers of the rest of us, skied her back to the guest house. Fortunately the injury did not turn out to be serious. Hitler expressed great interest in the ankle, a sure sign that he needed a drink and we duly obliged him, before, regretfully, saying "Auf Wiedersehen" and staggering upstairs to pack.

The long journey across Europe was not a pleasing prospect, but having said farewell to the Hechenmoos, we concentrated our minds on the return. The train rumbled towards Basel. That journey, with short breaks here and there, was to go on for thirty-six hours, but it turned out to be a pleasant experience.

A first class meal was served to all on the train and this in itself took a considerable slice out of the trip. It started off inauspiciously enough with an apple and this was followed by tomato soup, fish in sauce, chicken and vegetables, a small round steamed pudding that tasted of dates and mixed herbs, and a portion of jam with it, chocolate gâteau and cheese and biscuits, all washed down with white wine of a surprisingly good quality. By the time the meal was over we were ready to slip onto the floor of the carriage and go flat out, and might have done so had not hot, strong coffee been brought round.

By the time Basel was reached, we had recovered sufficiently to get our cases together and wobble onto the platforms to change trains. The second leg home was through Switzerland and France to Calais and for this we were provided with couchettes which were the actual seats we were sitting on, skilfully manoeuvred by the porters in a matter of seconds.

We were very tired, but whilst Josie and the two other passengers we shared the compartment with slept soundly, I could not so much as doze off. I gazed for hours out of a chink of the window blind, at scenery that hardly ever changed. To relieve the boredom, I swung myself down on the floor three or four times, stepping carefully so as not to wake anybody, and walked up and down the corridor. It was astonishing, not to say alarming, to find some of the outward carriage doors swinging in the wind as the train lurched along. Whatever else I thought about British Rail, I knew that sort of thing could not happen in England.

At eight o'clock the porter came round bawling out in French and the couchettes were soon converted back into seats. Everyone freshened up and got out books, packs of cards and pocket chess sets. Breakfast was, as usual, the continental roll and butter with coffee or chocolate. A whole day had passed.

Painfully slowly the train chugged on, passing towns and villages where figures waited on the platforms for their own local connections and at last we arrived at the harbour station which by contrast, was a hive of activity.

The news was not good. The cross-channel ferry was held up by high winds and was not expected to dock for four hours. Those were the longest hours, for we could not help thinking that perhaps it would not turn up at all and it was miserable standing about waiting hopefully but not optimistically. There was a great rush for it when it finally tied up and we were so glad that it unloaded and took on its fresh passengers and mail in very quick time indeed.

Nevertheless, many passengers were left behind including some unlucky souls who had elected to make a short stroll into Calais.

The nearer we got to Dover the colder it became. Crouched below deck for most of the journey we felt a great longing for England and our home. Josie was looking pale and worn out. The passage of time slowed up again, for when we got to Dover there was another long delay before the London train eased out.

To judge by the way it so slowly ground forward, with the points flashing blue beneath the wheels, the frequent stops for reasons we could only guess at and the desolate fields of snow we passed, we had come back to chaos.

"Are you still of the opinion that 1963 will be a good year?" Josie enquired, giving me a long searching look as if I might say 'no'.

"Why not?" I wearily replied, "Why not?"

What a strange question to ask at the end of a holiday.

X

It was eight p.m. and it seemed a year and a half instead of a day and a half away from Innsbruck.

Our cases stood on the ground beside us and the weather, if anything, was colder. There were few people about and those that were hurried along huddled up and silent. It was the all-pervading damp that crept underneath our alpine clothes, that and the weariness of the all-night travel. I picked up a case in each hand and prepared for the last short stage of the journey. Josie looked me full in the face, and said,

"I think I'm pregnant."

Never the one to express inward reactions, I nodded acquiescence that I had heard and understood her remark, but on the short walk home a whole array of thoughts and emotions jostled together. Flash bang. With those four words had gone - for the foreseeable future if not forever - all our plans for individual independence, leaving behind the murky grey cloud of sameness and conformity.

I was thinking, too, of events in the recent past that had shaken the world into a crisis for the third time in fifteen years, the almighty mushroom cloud that would kill off the creature, man, for a hundred maybe a thousand, years. The Cuban Missile Crisis, following the Suez/Hungary near disaster and The Berlin Airlift, had made all people tremble. The fatalistic outlook, voluntary or otherwise, was enough to sustain the individual adult, but - what a world to bring an unsuspecting child with an unsullied soul into.

The Kennedy-Khrushchev confrontation was vivid in the memory. Pop had sat in our lounge smoking one cigarette after another listening to each and every news bulletin, whilst I had argued that the holocaust, if it came, would take everyone, leaders and led alike, by complete surprise. Perhaps from out of a clear sky on a Good Friday or a Christmas Day, or maybe as we slept in our beds - who could say? - would fall that evil object, and mankind would vanish.

However one looked at it, any child born in the second half of the twentieth century would exist on the flimsiest of premises, namely, that man could live at peace with himself, and would be intelligent enough and tolerant enough to control his destiny.

True it was, that each generation had its problems. Pop's had had two world wars and mass unemployment, and his parents had survived diseases, now almost extinct, but which in their time had killed. Diphtheria and Scarlet Fever, to mention but two, had mown down thousands, and going back further, inadequate hospitals, operations without anaesthetics, dirt and poverty had reigned.

Lucky to be alive today? Perhaps it was an arguable point.

As for us, we were due to move and it was only the proposed sale of The Prado that was holding things up. It was now far from sure that the decision we had taken a few months before had been the right one. It would be an almighty upheaval as these things mostly are, and although the Isleworth house had given every token of being in first class shape, there was bound to be plenty of work to be done getting the place the way we wanted it. Of a surety, too, the loss of Josie's income would be felt in full measure.

We had always been good savers without stinting ourselves to the bone, and if we had had occasionally to rough it, there had always been an end in view.

"Well?" said my wife, as we strode along.

"Well, what?"

"Most husbands say how pleased they are."

"Do they?"

"So I believe."

"All I can say is, 'Congratulations'. I'm not surprised at your news but don't mention anything to Nana, will you?"

"I didn't intend to."

"And don't count your chickens before they're hatched."

Josie laughed but whether it was because the idea was absurd or whether it was at me I did not know. We turned the corner into our street and were met by a pretty grim sight, for unlike the main road it was a mass of dirty solid rutted snow, with every few yards a car standing, forlorn and dejected, objects that summed up the winter.

On the pavements at regular intervals were stem pipes for emergency water supply. It was as bad as that. A solitary dog wandered past us looking cold and hungry and I hoped that he had not been put out for the night. The lights from the curtained windows looked dimmer than they should have and the music from the radios and televisions was muted. It was not the way we had hoped or expected to return from a winter's holiday at a place that revelled in snowy conditions.

At last we turned the key in the lock, dumped our cases in the passage, wiped our feet and strode into the lounge. Immediately our spirits lifted at the sight of a great roaring fire that threw its heat across the room to us. Nana was sitting at the table playing patience and Smokey was recumbent on an armchair.

It was a most welcoming sight. He opened one eye as if to say, 'So you've decided to come home have you?' Then he surveyed us for some seconds with his tail moving slightly backwards and forwards. After that, he stretched himself in the typical feline manner, jumped down and came over to us.

"He's missed you," Nana said after we had exchanged greetings with her. "He's been off his food, I'm afraid, though I've tried him on liver. The kettle's on and I'll soon get a cup of tea going."

"It's not the usual raptures we get from Mokey," I said, "but he's pleased enough," and so he was. I noted, however, that his fur had become very knotted in our absence, and resolved that if we ever got another cat it would not be a Persian. His nose was as pink as ever, and when we stroked him, his fur crackled with static.

As we took off our coats and thawed out, Nana bustled around in the kitchen. Our hands and feet were tingling. We were together again, the three of us, and Nana was the guest.

I was surprised to find that the Austrian sun had got at our faces, for the sunburn was severe in places and our necks were sore.

Turning to Nana who had got together a mixed grill and hot cups of tea, I enquired as to which bed Mokey had slept on.

"Neither," she said. "His favourite spot has been the armchair."

"And how's everything in the house?"

"Not too bad. There's one burst in the bathroom. You'll have to get that seen to or do without a bath. Otherwise things are exactly as you left them."

I heaved a sigh of relief.

"Any post?"

She handed me over six or seven letters, only one of

them important. It was from the Estate Agents to say that a Mr. Smith would be calling round the following day to look over the house. We had had many such messages before without anything coming of them so I was only mildly hopeful.

'There is no urgency about the business any more,' I told myself. 'What is to be will be.' The only vital question concerned the future possible hatching, but not a hint was dropped to Nana before she departed the following morning. We were truly grateful to her for having done such a fine job.

Mr. Smith turned up at the appointed hour and said his wife was leaving the matter completely to him. He made copious notes in a pocket book and went; a tall, silent man who refused refreshment.

"I bet you, despite what he said, his missus will want to see the place," Josie said. "No-one can be so under a man's thumb as to not want to see her future home," but she was wrong.

A letter arrived from the agents mentioning an offer close enough to our asking price to be considered and after a bit of to-ing and fro-ing a deal was concluded. Unfortunately, by that very post, a letter from Mr. and Mrs. Vince's solicitor stated that they could wait no longer and if a completion date could not be agreed within ten days, the sale was off. Whether this was as definite as it sounded was open to question, but we took it at its face value.

We were both in a fatalistic frame of mind hoping that the whole matter would be solved by the course of events, but the letter needed a reply and there was no point in prevarication, which itself was a form of subtle motivation.

Looking at the grim weather, the thought of moving was ridiculous, but it would – surely - change. On the other hand, The Prado had always been a cold house despite the draught-proofing of every door and window, and the modern Isleworth residence, which we had been given to understand had been a show house when the street was originally built, had been well looked after. Maybe a little too much - for we had had it surveyed and the report had been short and very favourable. Then again we had had difficulty in finding a buyer for our home and now we had one. It was the crunch.

It is odd how one can get attached to an old house, and ours was without a doubt interesting and individualistic, so that although it had its faults, we quickly overlooked them because of our basic liking for the place. In parting, it would do us the best of good turns in that we would be able to show a profit that could go straight into a building society and continue to work for us, a kind of repayment for what we had done for it.

Modern houses are seldom so interesting but they give less trouble.

Other questions that flittered through our minds were the possibility that Mr. Smith would be unable to get a mortgage and maybe there was a whole line of people buying and selling houses and all waiting approvals from someone, so if the chain broke all would fail. Also the chances of getting a bridging loan had been mooted.

In the end we tossed a coin and hoped for the best. As Willie Shakespeare so aptly put it, 'There's a divinity that shapes our ends, Rough-hew them how we will'

We wrote stating that we would go ahead and the date fixed was the 30th March. We carried on exactly as we had always done, going to work for five days of the week, doing odd jobs in the house, going to the theatre, relaxing before the television in front of the fire and attending our adult education classes.

The memory of our winter holiday soon faded but the

winter itself did not, or if it did, it was so slow as to be hardly noticed, but one morning I looked at the buds of the overhanging branches of next door's apple tree and noticed that they had swelled. We were so pleased to see this sure sign of the end of the siege, glad too for the sake of the birds who had first welcomed us to the house. We had done our best for them but they had had a rough time.

Despite the bread and water regularly put out for them, it was not uncommon for one of us to go out in the morning and find frozen bodies on the path. We lost count of the number which must have been in excess of twenty, all buried in a communal grave at the bottom of the garden.

Spring did eventually arrive and with it a dramatic transformation. In no time at all the forsythia bushes that could be seen in most gardens were ablaze with golden blossom and we resumed our Sunday morning jaunts into Kew Gardens.

We received a delightful little note from Mrs. Vince wishing us good luck in her old (and what would be our new) home and replied in suitable tones.

I had seen our bank manager who had explained in detail the terms of a bridging loan he would grant us. The deeds and documents of the Isleworth house arrived and were eagerly perused.

The house had been built in the early thirties and had only had three owners. The Vinces had been there for twelve years. For a short period we were the owners of the two houses, in the transfer waiting months, and as I jokingly remarked to Josie, could be classed as bloated capitalists. This was far from the truth for the overdraft meant we were 'in the red' and when all was settled we would be no more than comfortable.

The sale of Mr. and Mrs. Vince's house concluded. With

the keys in our possession, I decided it would be prudent to make an inspection and if there was any small thing to be done to make a note of it so that when we moved in, we would know what was required.

With the snow thawing, that unbelievably well-kept garden would at least have to be brought up to scratch, the grass cut, the rose beds weeded and the paths swept, but I had no intention of devoting more than the minimum of time to it. When the last vestige of snow had disappeared and the sun was shining, I put the key into the bright blue front door lock and stepped into the empty house.

It was Saturday morning and as I opened the door and stepped into the hallway, I recalled that other morning at Richmond. Closing the door I went to the stairs and ascended. To my amazement I found a bird flying about in the back bedroom.

It was not one I recognised as my bird recognition did not go far beyond the sparrow, the blackbird and the robin, but I was mightily puzzled as to how it had got there. There were no fireplaces on the top floor, no entrance or exit to a loft, the grates on the ground floor were blocked up and the back entrance firmly locked. I made a desultory effort to catch the bird, then decided to shoo it downstairs, which, after an effort, I succeeded in so doing.

Opening the back door, I waited for the bird to fly out. It showed no desire to, but circled the room as if it were a budgerigar or a canary. Exasperated, I took off my pullover and chased it about until at last I wafted it into the garden where it stayed on a branch for approximately five seconds and flew back in again.

It took me half an hour to get that bird back to its natural environment leaving me to sit down on the floor exhausted. The only explanation I was ever to arrive at about that particular incident, was that Mr. or Mrs. Vince had been back to their house weeks after the sale was completed and had inadvertently allowed the intruder in.

With nothing in it, the house looked entirely different from the last time I had seen it, but it did not have a neglected air. It was now apparent that there was no cupboard space but there were a number of niches that could be converted, and the house itself was immaculately clean. Apart from the essentials, such as bath and hot water heater, the place had been stripped of almost everything that could be regarded as a fixture or a fitting. Even the light bulbs had been taken. Just one convenience item had been left behind in a corner of the front room - a telephone.

The greenhouse looked as if it had been newly painted, but the garden was already reverting to its natural state. I knew I would have to come over again with shears and a lawnmower, but all in all I was well pleased. Josie and I would have an easy time of it, but before we moved, it would have to become a regular habit to call at the Isleworth house to keep it trim, and we would be able to bring over small articles and stow them. The door leading from the greenhouse to the garden would be an ideal place for me to prepare a cat-flap entrance for Mokey.

When I got back to Richmond, I found that Josie had been having some excitement with birds, too. That tree whose roots were so firmly planted in next door's garden and whose branches so invitingly sprawled into ours, had become the home of a blackbird and his mate. In late May the tree had blossomed in all its glory, the flowers had faded, and hanging out some washing Josie had glanced across and seen the nest being built.

We had both become accustomed to our feathered friends fetching and carrying little bits of straw and twigs but it was the first time either of us had seen the task at close hand.

Josie carried on with her work until a sudden squawking and screeching drew her attention again to the nest. What she saw was the nest with the two birds circling around kicking up their din, whilst Smokey was sitting on a branch a yard or so away peering benignly at what was going on.

Whether it was the mother's or the father's idea to build the nest so low could not be determined but both were now doing their utmost to divert the cat's attention elsewhere. Those birds need not have worried and heaven's fury from them could have been saved, but Josie lifted Smokey down and took him into the house so that they could get on with their task.

The birds may have been foolish to build their nest where cats could get at it, but having started they were determined to finish it. Perhaps time was short, for not many days had passed when investigations revealed that there were five tiny bluish-green eggs on the soft moss. The mother bird did not sit on her nest all the while so we were able to keep an eye on it. That the inevitable would happen and cause a problem occupied our minds and Mokey, however good-natured, had to be kept away from the scene.

Sure enough the eggs hatched out and a matter of hours later we heard the howls of anger from the parents again. Rushing out we found the chicks on the ground and a cat - not ours I'm glad to say - running across the garden. The nest was in ruins and the parents were at panic stations. The tiny creatures were no more than balls of fluff and although their little mouths were opening and closing, no sound came from them. We carried them indoors and placed them on a piece of rag in a cardboard box whilst cogitating a plan that, although not foolproof, might work.

Above a small side window halfway up the wall of the house, I fixed two large nails and with an effort managed to secure a plastic laundry basket to them. Cloth was put in the bottom and the remains of the nest secured and placed thereon. The infant birds were then carried up a ladder and so put back in something like their nest and this time away from predatory felines.

Above the laundry basket I rigged up an umbrella to keep the rain out and we waited for the parents' reaction. It did not take very long for the mother and father to find their fledglings and soon they were both feeding them, a spectacle which gave us much interest and enjoyment.

The baby blackbirds prospered and grew feathers and squawked louder. The parents were flying to and fro with food all day long. Each morning I climbed the ladder and peered over to see how they were getting on, and so it was that one day I found one of the little birds perched on the edge of the basket with its body puffed out like a balloon. It eyed me suspiciously for a couple of minutes, then swooped away with a flurry of wings to disappear into the distance. The first flight of a blackbird and I was thankful and proud that I had helped to send it on its way.

That left four and not many days later on there was only one. We christened him Willie for obvious reasons and when he passed a further week on his own, we felt sure something was wrong with him. Mother and Father continued to feed him, screeching at us if we were in the way. Although he puffed himself out to the full like his brothers and sisters, Willie could not make it. Twice we found him on the ground and each time returned him to his nest.

One evening there was a storm with heavy rainfall and when it was over, we went out and found poor Willie in the drain where doubtless he had been washed along the guttering. We, of course, read portents into the whole episode. The blackbirds had shown us how universal was nature's instinct for the preservation of the specie. It was a reminder of basic values. It was a good example of how the male and female should undertake parenthood. I said, "It means, Josie, that you will have quads."

Mokey knew something was up long before the packing to move was done. Perhaps he thought we were going away and leaving him for another week. In the hustle of the final preparations he almost got overlooked, but when we caught sight of him sitting dejectedly on the floor just as he had been when first we had met him, we knew we had to reassure him that all was well. We fussed over him till he perked up. Yet he remained irritated with our preoccupation, and would scratch at the furniture to draw attention to himself. When he saw we noticed him, he would give us a fixed look of satisfaction. If we scolded him his tail would shoot upwards with pleasure.

As the time for our departure got close, he became listless and we ascribed it to his keen feline psychic sense of forthcoming unwanted events, the possible benefits of which he could not appreciate. We knew that most cats loved their homes as much as they loved their master and mistress, and I recalled tales of cats who had walked miles with unerring sense of direction to their old abodes. Cats might have limited intelligence but they are uncannily resourceful if the situation demands it.

It was a common sight those days to see Mokey in the garden, chewing away at the grass, considered to be a cat's medicine, but he had done it often enough before and the only result had been that he had sicked up fur, which was probably the required thing.

As we now know, looking after a long-haired cat is not easy. There is constant combing, the regular inspections for knots of fur, the powdering, the de-infesting. Mokey did his fair share in keeping himself clean, but the job was beyond him and so he continually swallowed fur, ate grass and was sick.

We decided to give him a thorough going over. Josie took him on her lap and spent almost an entire evening cutting, combing and powdering and when she had finished he looked quite splendid, but I noticed he had taken little interest in the proceedings, nor did he apply himself with his usual vigour to the task of getting rid of any surplus powder. I presumed it was a case of familiarity breeding, maybe not contempt but perhaps boredom.

He went off his food for a while which was not unusual for him but it lasted longer than it had done before. Cats, as is well known, are creatures of moods and whether sick in mind or body do not complain, but tend to withdraw into themselves till they feel better. Not unlike some human beings.

I picked him up one evening and fancied he had got thinner. It was a worrying thought so, with the aid of a shopping basket and a spring balance, I weighed him. He was two pounds under what he should have been, so to be on the safe side we decided to take him to a vet. Our friendly local newsagent recommended a man at Hounslow. We had already purchased a cat basket preparatory to the big move so it was a simple matter to place him in it and catch the bus.

It was the first time I had been in the waiting room of a Veterinary Surgeon, which was exactly the same as that of a doctor's except that there was a good deal more conversation going on. Pets apparently excited more interest than humans. The cats, of which there were three, included a Siamese that lay peacefully on its mistress's lap. There were also four or five dogs, a canary, a budgerigar, and a hamster which a small boy had in a box clutched tightly to him.

The only person who did not speak in that crowded room was a tall and bulky man who must have weighed every bit of eighteen stones. He held an Alsatian dog on a lead, and when a woman enquired what was wrong with the animal, he said nothing in reply except shake his head and fumble in his pocket for cigarettes.

When his turn to see the vet came he stubbed out his cigarette, tapped the dog's head and followed the lady assistant into the surgery. A long, long wait followed, and everyone gazed at the closed door when any slight sound was heard. The waiting room became unbearably crowded and there was a hubbub of conjecturing concerning the man and his dog.

Silence suddenly descended on the room as the vet's voice could be heard talking to the man, then the door opened and the man came out, alone. Clutching the lead in his hand and looking neither to right or left he slowly traversed the room and went out into the night. I am sure that each and every one of us felt a little sadness on his behalf.

Then it was Mokey's turn and I entered the surgery with him, thrusting aside the vague ridiculous thought that he would meet the same fate as the dog, whatever that was. Round the walls of the large room were built-in kennels and cat cupboards, some of which were occupied, but there was no sign of the Alsatian.

The vet was a middle-aged man of florid countenance, not the sort of face to inspire confidence, and I had misgivings about having brought Mokey there. Having placed our cat on a table, he prodded him in various parts of his body.

He did not stroke him or say anything to him, nor did he ask me any questions. When I explained that Mokey's listlessness was causing us concern, he remarked, "He's a Persian. It's to be expected." He then pressed Mokey's mouth open, gazed down it with the help of his assistant's torch and announced "Two bad teeth. They will have to come out."

My spirits fell but I agreed to the extraction, expecting the creature to be given an anaesthetic, but not so. I did not know much about these matters and watched in horrified silence as the teeth were yanked out and put in a bucket. I saw no sign of instruments being sterilised. As for Mokey - he had been silent up to the moment of extraction, when his terrified mews filled the room. In a bit of a daze myself, I heard the vet mutter to me to see the assistant about payment. Like the big man before me I went through the waiting room staring straight ahead, but at least I had the cat with me.

I was so relieved to get out of the place, and had the fervent hope that the vet had known what he was doing, and that it was for the best, and that Mokey would now get back to his old self.

Josie was on tenterhooks when I returned and when I told her about the teeth, blamed herself for not giving him enough bone to chew on and for cutting up his meat too small and for giving him too much tinned food.

In actual fact, as far as a cat's diet went, Mokey had done reasonably well. He had a fair share of rabbit and chicken bones, fish both raw and cooked, mince meat, lamb's hearts and cat cereal, plus his favourite - pilchards in tomato sauce. As for the tins, they were supposed to contain all the necessary vitamins for a cat's good health.

It took Mokey a few days to get over his ordeal, but we were glad to note that he got his appetite back and took an interest in things again. If he still looked quizzically at our piled-up furniture, it was not the unhappy look he had worn before. We decided that the vet with the brusque manner and somewhat slovenly mode of operation must, after all, have known his job.

The summer was in full swing as Mother Nature made up for lost time, and people, too, threw off their cares and smiled at the world as they breathed the perfumed air of the parks and gardens. What a different picture the Thames presented with its swans sailing gaily along followed by their broods, and pleasure boats plying their trade upstream and downstream. Instead of ice, the order of the day was ice-cream.

We eventually left The Prado before the sale was finally completed, enabling us to visit it before it became the property of Mr. Smith, and we were quite sad about it. There would be no more delicious apples from that prolific and obliging tree, no more looks out of the bedroom window at that quaint and friendly-looking pagoda and the Sunday visits to Kew Gardens would be gravely curtailed. True we were not going very far, just a bus ride away from Richmond and the walks "up by the river, down by the green" as we had often put it. Nostalgia held us in its sway. The house had had our undivided attention for the last few years. It held many memories and a lot of ourselves had gone into it. Things would never be quite the same again.

With Mokey safely in his basket, we got into the big pantechnicon and journeyed off through Richmond town, over the bridge and so through East Twickenham and St. Margaret's to Isleworth. The men had instructions to place everything save the essentials into the front room. It was all labelled up as to where it had to go and we were determined to sort it out at our leisure.

There are various theories as to how one should treat a cat on moving day. For our part we turned his basket round three times before we left and repeated this when we arrived, the object being to confuse the cat's sense of direction. It made more sense than the butter on the paws theory.

The house we moved to was eminently different from the one we left but in due course we would make the adjustments. There was no need of a cat-run unless another animal of the Sylvester type came on the scene which was unlikely, and I had already fitted up the cat-flap.

The rose bushes were in full bloom, dominating the outlook from right to left and from back to front. I could not but help noting how all the gardens in the road were kept so beautifully and the lawns were without exception in first class order. It was one of those areas where the great majority took more than an average interest in horticulture and I knew that, although no slouch myself when it came to hoeing and weeding, I could never emulate them.

The outlook was prettiness itself, although it lacked the appeal of the silent pagoda; but, there it was, we would have to get used to it. We unpacked our reproduction self-portraits and hung them in every room, giving a bare semblance of continuity.

It was a different area right enough, for within an hour of arriving the neighbours were knocking on the front door, asking us if there was anything we wanted to know and promptly giving us the information such as where the nearest bus stop was, when the dustmen called, and the best time to catch the milkman.

On the first Sunday we walked down to South Street, through Railshead Road to the river, along the bridge that led to The Old Deer Park, then back via the town and the bridge and it was a walk that was to be the first of many.

Mokey settled in easily enough. We kept him in for the first day and then opened the back door to see what he would do. He sniffed the step and the ground outside, was apparently satisfied and wandered off into the garden.

At night he sat on the grass gazing with bliss at all around him, ears cocked for new sounds. It was as if he were dreaming of his cat's heritage, reverting to the times when it was essential for the survival of their specie to be both alert and relaxed at the same moment. A pleasurable combination while it lasted, belonging only to his kind. Cats in the comparative safety of the modern world, where owners often pandered to their every whim, sometimes lost for a while that other sweet taste of life itself.

Perhaps because he had been doctored as a kitten, there was little of the prowling, hunting tom in Mokey, but he loved to pretend. I do not think he ever attacked another cat in his life and if the occasional Sylvester-type cat had a go at him he would make a hasty retreat.

There was one feline who entered our house unexpectedly by way of the cat-flap, a contrivance he must have been familiar with. It was a largish black animal with one white whisker. He was a friendly creature who padded over to us and rubbed his head against our legs. Mokey watched him with interest and did not show any hostile reaction even though the intruder went over to his saucers and devoured the contents.

"He's looking for a home," Josie said.

"Maybe, but whoever gave him the message got it wrong. There's no place for him here and if there was, we are not having Mokey's nose put out of joint. Besides, he looks well fed." I laughed. "He's like the neighbours - visiting us because we're new."

The animal turned up in the garden two or three times as friendly as before but we determined not to feed it or encourage it in any way.

Just one month after our arrival, when we were just getting used to things, we had a rude shock. Indeed, as we went happily about our tasks we had not the slightest idea that slings and arrows would be landing on our doorstep. We had been out shopping together on a Saturday morning and, returning with our bags and parcels, opened the front door to discover a scene of utter confusion.

A cupboard I had put in the hallway had had its doors ripped off and the contents strewn on the floor. Further investigation revealed that each room had been vandalised by one or more intruders, but nothing had been taken. They must have been looking for money and in their rage at not finding any had wrecked the rooms.

How long they had been there we could only guess at. It was probable that our return had upset their plans, for the only item of any value that we possessed was the television and that was still there and intact.

A panel of the greenhouse door had been smashed enabling them to turn the lock and gain entrance. Despite their frustration, they must have worked silently for when we asked the next door neighbours if they had seen or heard anything, they answered that they had not, and if Mokey had seen what had happened, he was not talking about it.

It was quite a blow to see the efforts of weeks reduced to nothing but, after our anger and bitterness had waned, we managed to look at the bright side. What was damaged was not valuable and we had left no money or important documents lying about. The police came round and gave the place a thorough dusting for fingerprints without finding any. We started the tiresome business of sorting out, rearranging and general clearing up.

I was sure that a burglar who wanted to get in would always do so, but to make it as difficult as possible, we had new locks fitted to the front and back doors and a metal panel placed over the vulnerable greenhouse exit. We were getting over this disturbing episode when another unfortunate and totally unexpected incident occurred and Josie began to have serious doubts that my prophecy that it would be a good year would be correct.

XI

Walking across the kitchen is not exactly where danger is anticipated, but I was doing just this one morning when I slipped and nearly crashed to the floor. It would have been better if I had fallen for in the effort to keep upright, I twisted to the side and felt a twinge of pain in my left leg. I thought no more about it until the next morning when I found it impossible to get to my feet and the pain was agonising.

Despite vigorous massaging, the leg did not improve in the slightest and reluctantly I had to admit that it would be impossible for me to go to work that day. With an effort of will I managed to get dressed and lay on the couch to await a doctor. The leg I balanced on a chair and I gritted my teeth as successive spasms of pain occurred. The doctor could not make up his mind what the matter was. He examined the leg for a long time before giving me a prescription for pain-killing tablets with the instruction that if it was no better on the morrow, he was to be telephoned immediately and I would probably have to go into hospital.

Again I enquired as to the exact nature of the injury but he said it could not be diagnosed without an x-ray and that was what I would have to have if there was no improvement.

"That's two things that's happened since we got here," Josie remarked. "There's bound to be a third."

"Pure gloomy superstition," I answered. "I'm perfectly O.K. That is, almost."

Three days of inertia followed, alleviated only by reading and watching the television. The injury was diagnosed as a badly pulled thigh muscle. I was determined to get to work the following Monday and our kind neighbours loaned me a walking stick. With the aid of this I set out.

It was not easy and time and time again I stopped with sweat pouring off of me with the effort. Although I got to work an hour late, I was elated for I knew I had conquered the pain and that the leg was on the mend. Nevertheless, I stopped at home again the following day and it was on this day that Josie's third thing came slowly into focus.

I was able to get about the house a bit and had contrived to pull the couch across the floor to the lounge window so that I could look out at the front garden and the street beyond. Thus idly glancing, my eyes chanced to alight on our Mokey. He was lying beneath the hedge that circumnavigated the house. This by itself was not unusual but from where I was his posture looked a little odd and I wondered what he was up to.

I could see some movement and opened the window and looked out. His body was curved in a shallow arc and he was moving backwards and forwards ever so slightly, rubbing his fur in the dust. Very intrigued, I limped slowly over to him and bending down surveyed his tiny shape. There was no doubt about it - he was giving his body a dust bath, for presently he turned over on the other side and repeated the movements. His behaviour puzzled me immensely especially as he had not reacted to my presence.

"Smokey! What are you up to?"

I stroked him and he looked up with an expression of complete disinterest, as if his tiny mind was concerned with far more important things than a fondle from a human being, no matter who he was. I stroked him again, then returned to the house nonplussed. I knew that birds habitually gave themselves a dust bath but I had never heard of a cat doing likewise.

The more I thought about it the unhappier I felt without

being able to say why. Every few minutes I looked out at him and although he moved his spot three times he remained in the dirt. Eventually I went out again, picked him up and brought him in. With a brush kept specially for him, I went over his fur, getting rid of the dust and a fair amount of fur also and he seemed pleased with the attention he was getting.

When Josie came in I said nothing about it. For one thing it would have worried her and for another, although I told myself it was probably a temporary aberration on Mokey's part, other more morbid thoughts intervened. I enquired of her if Mokey was eating much.

"Very little," my wife answered. "It's a waste of time buying food for him. He pecks at what's put down. Might eat a bit here and there but mostly leaves it. Except for his pilchards, that is. Haven't you noticed?"

"I must confess I haven't. I suppose I've been so wrapped up with my, shall I say, affliction that I've hardly noticed anything that's going on. I hope he's not getting sick again."

"It's probably the hot weather."

It was just two days later that Josie noticed Mokey acting oddly again. She came rushing into the house with a startled look.

"What's up?"

"It's Mokey. He's under a rose bush and it looks as if he's trying to bury himself."

"Or a bone," I suggested. "I always said he was a bit dog-like."

It was a feeble attempt at a joke to dispel the alarm I felt.

"Come and look!"

Sure enough he was beneath a bush and was pushing his

little head into the soft earth, not frantically, but with a sure, deliberate, painstaking motion. At that moment, the black cat arrived in the garden and Mokey desisted, looked at him, then resumed his peculiar occupation.

"He's trying to bury himself," Josie said.

"What! Commit suicide? Utter nonsense and you know it."

"I didn't mean that. It - it's as if he's trying to return to the earth from which he and all things come."

"What a morbid thought!"

Despite my words, I had exactly the same impression as she had, and it was with a sense of foreboding that we went back indoors.

"What's to be done, Theo?"

"I am not taking him back to that butcher of a vet. No. That quack won't touch him. Take out some more teeth and pronounce him fit. The man ought to see a doctor himself."

"He did improve after he went there."

"Yes, but for how long? Anyway, I'm by no means convinced that his teeth were any more than a nuisance to him. Bring him in and we will look for ourselves."

We held him on a table underneath a lamp, prised his mouth open and with the aid of a torch looked into his mouth. Mokey obediently submitted to his jaws being opened. His tail rose in the air at the attention he was being given and I wondered if, perhaps, we had not been giving him as much fussing as we should have during the moving business and subsequent events, for he was a sensitive cat.

Dismissing this idea as being too extravagant, I spoke. We'll find another vet. His teeth look O.K. but we'll make sure - about everything."

"I'll take him. You're not fit."

"Right. Pop next door and ask Mrs. Jones if she knows of anybody. She's got a little dog so it should be a good recommendation."

The neighbour gave us the details of a local vet but said she had never had occasion to go there herself so could not say whether she was any good. We decided to wait a couple more days and managed to get Mokey to take some vitamin tablets with his milk which he still eagerly drank.

He was particularly fond of condensed milk and as well as this, we tempted him with boiled fish, liver and pilchards. He ate very little and his general lack-lustre approach to things was not encouraging.

On the Saturday, he was still spending most of his leisure lying in the earth, but was not rubbing himself in it. We cleaned him up, put him in his basket and Josie took him off for a second opinion. She was gone a long time and I kept thinking of the man and the dog in the other waiting room. When she returned Josie was in a rage.

"An absolutely ruddy waste of time," she declared. "The woman's a fraud. Didn't bother to examine him and I had waited for ages. She said he was an old cat and could do nothing for him except give him vitamin tablets. All the old witch is after is the customer's money. She's not the least bit interested in cats or dogs or anything else. I've a good mind to report her!"

"She said he was an old cat?"

"That's what she said, and she said he should be put to sleep."

"Well, we know Mokey's eight and even in cat years that

doesn't make him an OAP. Besides his features are still young-looking even though he's under the weather. That's that then. Another quack vet. We'll just have to find one who is properly qualified. I find it hard to believe that these people can set up in business without a sense of vocation, but there it is."

"Poor Mokey. Everything's going against him."

"There's one thing you can do at once, Josie. Ring up your father and see what he says. Pop's had a world of experience of all sorts of cats and ought to be able to at least give us some advice."

Pop's words were comforting. "There's obviously something wrong with him," he said, "but it may be nothing much. However, it's best to be on the safe side. If you can't find a good vet, I'll come down and fetch him back here. The chap we go to is absolutely splendid and people come from miles around to see him. For now I should keep him indoors as much as possible and make sure he's warm. Keep an eye on him in case he's sick and let him have plenty of water to drink."

There was no more we could do that day, and, hoping that it was all a passing phase such as both cats and humans go through, we went to bed in a happier frame of mind than we had done for several days. Nevertheless, the picture-image of Mokey lying in the earth was not a happy one to go to sleep with.

Sunday was a bright autumn day such as often occurs in England, as if the late season was trying to make sure that all things had prospered to their appropriate degree.

We had not set the alarm and Mokey had failed to wake us for the first time for weeks. He was curled up on Josie's bed and I leaned over and stroked him.

Was he only under the weather? Was he feeling his age? Or was he genuinely sick?

He had been pretty healthy on the whole since we had first had him except for the fleas and the mass of fur that so impeded him. There was no cat flu going about nor did he look as if he had a complaint of this nature. His coat had a sheen on the back, but he was undeniably thinner.

I raised his head and the mournful face, so unlike the full-of-interest, ultra-inquisitive face we knew so well, gave me the answer. There was a gentle purring.

"Good cat."

He stretched himself, flopped, not jumped, to the floor and padded over to his milk. He drank the lot and went off downstairs, through his cat-flap and out into the garden.

On the Monday we would go to the local library and get a list of all the veterinary surgeons there were in the neighbourhood and hopefully, it would be a case of third time lucky. We should at least find out what actually was the matter with him. Not knowing, hoping for the best and fearing the worst was not an ideal stance to take.

I made tea and woke Josie and we talked for a long while about the ailing Mokey. When we went out to look for him we expected to find him lying in the earth as before and so he was, but he had gone a step further. He had hollowed out a patch into a shallow depression and was curled up in it on his side with his tail between his paws. It was a common enough posture except that his head was sunk lower than his body.

"I don't like it," Josie said for the sixth time that morning.

"No more do I. We will leave him there for now, but later on I'll go over him again. Who knows? Perhaps he has an internal injury and he finds some alleviation from it by lying on the ground. Animals often know what's best for themselves."

"True, but we mustn't fuss him about too much. We might only make the matter worse. He probably wants to be left alone."

"Yes. When I've had a bad cold or the flu, all I've wanted is to stay in bed with no disturbances from friend or foe."

The morning was dominated by endless and pointless discussion about the animal. It was a problem we could not solve. We hurried through lunch hoping that he would come padding in and allow our companionship to perk him up a little, but as he did not, I went out in the mid-afternoon and fetched him.

Again I stood him on a table and carefully felt all over for bumps, swellings or cuts, anything that would give us a clue to his state. I actually hoped I would touch a tender spot and that he would react with a mew, or a frenzied jump, or a bite (a thing he had never done to us or to anyone). Apart from a gentle purr he stayed quiescent.

"What a wonderful patient!" I exclaimed. "But I give up!"

I turned to face Josie who had been watching anxiously. She uttered a gasp and cry of anguish. I heard a thud and looked back at Mokey. He had fallen on his side and was looking at us with pleading in his eyes.

"Good grief!" I said and felt my blood pressure rapidly rising.

Josie picked him up and cradled him in her arms. I racked my brains for a quick answer, for it was now a case of not being able to wait any longer, not even till the following morning.

"The PDSA," I said. "They will know what to do," and I rushed to find the telephone directory. I found the number within minutes, got through immediately and explained the situation. They gave me the number of an emergency vet and I repeated the story of what had happened. A cool masculine voice at the other end of the line made sympathetic responses, saying that he would be round in an hour, and we were not to do anything till he got there. I sighed with relief.

Mokey was placed on a settee with a blanket over him and a half-filled hot water bottle at his rear. He had a queer kind of amused look on his countenance, or so we thought. As if he was saying, 'What funny people you are. It's very good of you to take this trouble but I don't need the blanket and bottle'.

We sat down to wait. In less than the hour the bell rang and Josie rushed to answer it. It was the vet and I could see at once that he knew what he was about. He picked him up gently, stroked him a few times then enquired, "How long has he been like this?"

He was youngish, about thirty, and strode purposefully about the room with his bag, inspiring confidence. I gave him the whole history of the case from the moment at The Prado when he was off his food and we noticed he was thinner.

"Do you mean to tell me," he said, "that when you took him to a vet, he took out teeth and said he would be all right?"

"That is exactly what happened."

He shook his head. "I don't understand it, and this woman said it was old age?"

"Yes. I can give you her name and address."

"Never mind. There's no sense in raking it up. Your cat in the natural course of things would have a few years yet to go. Barring accidents, of course. Well, bad teeth don't help either."

He took out a stethoscope and tested various parts of Mokey's anatomy, felt him in much the same way as I had, and looked in his mouth and ears.

"I would have thought that a trained surgeon could have diagnosed this," he said. "I'll say no more. It's not ethical."

"What is the trouble, then?"

"Jaundice."

"How bad?"

"Pretty bad, I'm afraid. It should have been treated weeks ago."

He turned and faced us." You want to save your pet?"

"Of course."

"Well, I'll be frank with you. He'll have to have injections and special tablets. They cost a lot of money and I'll have to visit regularly for some weeks."

"And then?"

"With luck you will have a healthy animal for years to come."

"I'm glad to hear it. Just give us some idea of how much the whole course will cost."

The figure of a hundred pounds was my estimate, a small figure if Mokey recovered.

"It could be fifty pounds or thereabouts." I looked across at Josie and she nodded.

"That will be all right. I'll pay you for this visit now and we're both very grateful to you."

"Five pounds will be enough."

When the transaction was settled he took a syringe and phials out of his bag and with great care he gently injected Mokey in three different parts of his body. Each time he did so, the little cat gave the barest of mews and Josie winced.

The instructions given to us were to let Mokey lie exactly where he was but without the bottle and blanket, this so that he would be completely relaxed and allow the drugs to work through.

"I'll call again tomorrow morning," he said. "He'll have to have further injections." He looked straight at us. "I can see how fond you are of your pet and I'll do what I can, but I can't promise anything. If only you had come to me in the first place, he would be as right as rain by now."

'If,' I thought, but thanked him once more. When he had gone we sat down and watched the small silent animal, stretched out now on his side.

"I'll take the day off tomorrow," Josie said. "That's if you are going in."

"I think I ought to. The leg is much better."

It was one of those days that seemed to go on for ages and when evening turned to night it dragged more than ever. At last it was time for bed and as we undressed, Mokey uttered a slight mew.

"He knows he can't go on our bed," I said. "I'll sit up with him."

"No. I will."

"No. You go to bed now and tomorrow you can take your turn."

"Very well. I'll do that. I'll make a flask of tea for you."

I told myself that the idea of sitting up for a cat was rather ridiculous, even though the cat was our pet, our Mokey. He was but an animal and there was nothing I could do for him, but I wanted to, all the same.

To convince myself that it was a logical decision, I thought of those country farmers and veterinary surgeons to whom it was part of the job. Their dedication, however, could not be faulted and must have taxed reserves of patience and resolve, that not all possess, not to mention the discomfort they endured.

As Mokey was in no state to visit the garden, Josie put down newspaper and earth in a corner of the room, just as she had done when first he had arrived at our home.

We left the light on and I drew up a chair beside the settee, lit a cigarette and waited.

Every twenty minutes or so, Mokey gave a faint mew and I told myself he was complaining because he was not on Josie's bed, then stroked him to reassure that all was well in his home. It was gone three when the intervals between the mews became more frequent and I decided to time them. When the intervals had decreased to ten minutes I became anxious but found a ready answer. The effect of the drugs was wearing off and it was natural that in his weakened state, Mokey would feel pain where the jabs had taken place.

At half past three Mokey stirred, opened his eyes and with an effort sad to see, flopped onto the floor and plodded toward the corner of the room where he relieved himself, then returned. The glazed look he gave me I attributed to extreme tiredness and I lifted him back onto the settee and laid him down again.

He purred and although it was faint, I thought it a hopeful

sign, but I now knew beyond any argument that it was a crisis night for him and hoped that the turning point would be reached and passed by the following day. The second visit of the vet would mark the first positive step in the recovery of Mokey.

By five o'clock the period between the mews had increased to twenty minutes again and I was particularly pleased when a full half hour passed. Once more I stroked him and noticed that his body was considerably cooler. Was this a good or a bad sign? Whilst I was wondering about this and looking at him under the bright light, I could see what was happening.

Coming out in all directions from the deep white fur of Mokey, were those old enemies of his, the pest of all long-haired cats, those minute crawling, jumping things - the fleas. The illusion that Mokey would get better went with them. I stood up and emitted a loud groan. Josie sat bolt upright immediately.

"What is it?"

For a few seconds, I paced the room and did not answer.

"What is it? How is he?"

Frustration and anger mingled with sorrow as I barked out the words I had no wish to utter.

"Mokey is dead."

"Are you sure?"

She stared at me in disbelief.

"Absolutely certain."

Josie came over to the settee and we both stared moodily at the creature that had so recently been our pet. The fleas, driven out of their warm home by Mokey's demise, had disappeared and would not survive for long, a fact that gave me morbid satisfaction. I hated them and was certain they had been a contributory factor in the sad event. Despite all Smokey's efforts and ours, they had succeeded and it would have been no use telling me at that moment that all creatures, however big or however small - even germs - desire to live in a habitat of their choice, to cling to self-preservation and to exist for the purpose for which they were ordained.

I could not do it but Josie did. She bent down and kissed Mokey.

"What shall we do with him?" I asked.

"He wanted to get back to the earth. Yet I feel he's too good to be buried in the ground. That's what Dad would do, I know. We must not be morbid about it. We must not moon about him. We never have. He's gone. That's all there is to it."

"Well?"

"We'll leave him for the vet to take away and think of him as he was in his prime. It did not last very long. Yes, I think that's best."

So we did. Before we left for work we took off his collar and name tag, wrapped him up in cellophane, placed him in a cardboard box with five pounds for the fee and a note to the vet saying that if it was any more we would pay it.

'Thank you for your effort. Would you please dispose of the body.'

We left the box outside the front door and went our ways.

XII

That Monday was a wretchedly gloomy day. I kept telling myself to concentrate on the job in hand and forget the sight of that dead animal, but I could not.

I thought of the many photographs we had taken of him in the happy days. Mokey rolling down the front steps on his belly; Mokey in a deck chair; Mokey running down the street to meet us with his body close to the ground; Mokey waiting hopefully on the concrete post in front of The Prado; Mokey in the snow. There were many more, but not enough. It was sad, sad that I would not see that creature again.

Josie, too, had a miserable day. We met at home as usual, ate our tea in silence, then went out for a walk. Although we had the telephone at home we decided to tell Pop the news from a coin-box booth. He was duly sympathetic and I could almost hear him silently saying, 'Yes, he crawled into your heart'.

It was unusual for us, but we went for a drink in a pub and it should have been an interesting evening, for the conversation around us was stimulating and about those things that interested us.

A bearded man and his girl were going on about the paintings in the Tate Gallery. More piquantly a couple at the next table were discussing arrangements for divorce from their respective partners. They held our attention for a minute or so.

"He was only a cat," I said.

"A very lovely one."

"Yes. Agreed. All the same he was but an animal. Animals do not have souls. Though we have lost a good, a splendid pet, one we were very fond of, we must not raise it to the level of a human being. Suppose, for instance, and heaven forbid, that it was your father or mother who died, then we should rightly feel a sense of great personal loss. That's for sure."

She did not answer.

"That is so, isn't it?"

"It is. You are absolutely correct. We must be grateful that it was not one of our parents, or anyone near and dear to us. Glad that it was only Mokey."

I am not sure if that was the right conversation we should have been having at that time. What I do know is that the tiredness of the previous night for both of us (for Josie had slept but fitfully) caught up with us, mixed up with Mokey's death. Poor Josie could contain herself no longer. She burst unashamedly into tears.

Since then, much water has flowed under Richmond Bridge. The memory of Smokey's death faded as do all sad memories, but it did not disappear. Now and then, sometimes happily, sometimes not, it is revived. It is, however, memories of his life, indeed of our life together, that retain a remarkable impression on both of us. Why this should be remains a shrouded mystery to me.

Some things are clear. We are and were independent folk, and with all his kind he was independent also. When we had moved into our first home together, he had joined us soon after. We were, in a sense, all part of the one episode, the setting up of a hopeful environment in which we could be a family together.

He had come from a happy home and because his owners emigrated had been uprooted from his Balham kittenhood and passed over to us. We for our part, had said farewell to living in London lodgings and the three of us as new mates had to get on with one another as friends.

After a rough start when we were fearful of losing him and he did not trust us, there had been a period of readjustment. We, as the superior humans, had had to control him for his own good during his 'running wild' days and in the course of time he had accepted the situation.

He was not, in my opinion, a particularly intelligent cat, but what endeared him to us as much as anything was that in his own small mind he thought the matter out and consciously decided to accept us for what we were. Thus on one occasion he forgave me for chastising him and did not transgress again.

We came to rely on this dominant factor of his character, the desire to be, not just a pet, but a friend in his own right. It conflicted with most of our experience of cats, the personal history of cats stretching back to childhood - nice cats, lovable cats, strongly individualistic cats, all kinds of cats, right up to Smokey.

Had we doted on him for want of something else to dote on? I think not. We went about our affairs and kept him in his place. He was not a little altar in our house for us to come home to, but right beside us in our endeavours. He sensed the relationship that should exist between caring humans and dependent felines and contributed positively towards it.

Some months later, we entered our old street and I half felt for the keys in my pocket to rattle, the signal that would have caused him to appear on the pavement and come running to meet us.

Nor had Smokey doted on us though I had attributed dog-like characteristics to him. His was a combination of feline, canine and odd little other features. He was a pretty cat and knew it. Even those people who positively abhorred felines tolerated him. He was gentle.

So, during those years there grew an affinity of spirits encompassing the natural desire of most creatures to like and be liked. On the one side two humans, and on the other a dumb animal, and the relationship worked for the benefit of all three.

Time, circumstance and the concatenation of events that we call more simply coincidence brought the three of us into close orbit, and it was a shame that the period was short, but such is life.

Surely, I say to myself, there is some lesson to be learned from this unique and happy experience and maybe we are still learning it.

Five further cats - Plud, Kimmy, Lucky, Ellie and Phantom - were all given the same care and attention as dear Smokey. The rearing of two children, plus all the changes that life brings to individuals and the changes in life itself - after all that followed - the cherished memory of that one unique feline persists. Nothing more.

Cats are animals. Unlike humans they do not possess souls. When they die, they die.

And yet?

Also available from Riverrun Press...

The Legend of Cairn by David Goble

> 'John, you are finished' he told himself over and over again, as, bound hand and foot, he lay on the floor of his prison.
>
> 'You are going to have terrible things done to you, you will be screaming for mercy that will not be given to you. Folk that you have known will be jeering you, and wishing you more pain, more agony, and when you pass out they will cheer, and try to get you to your senses so that they can jeer again. And then, soon you will be no more – just a body to be cut up and put in the earth. Gone, and only remembered as a filthy beast.'

In medieval Jorvik, John the Dumb is condemned to death for a crime he did not commit.

His end will come on the following morning.

Rescued by the Ethereal Woman in White he leaves his prison. 'Go north,' says the lady and so he does. After many a faltering step he reaches Cairn and in the process creates a legend that lives on long after him. (157 pages) £7.95

Sandy's Holiday by Josie Goble

For 9-10 year old girls

In Looe, Cornwall, Sandy was enduring the worst holiday of her life.

Still missing her long-departed father, she had little money and was stuck with boring Gina. Then, as if things could not get any worse, she had slipped and suffered a stupid accident.

Now Sandy finds she must learn to see things through different eyes and discovers a far more wonderful world than she ever dreamed possible.

(78 pages) £6.50

On the Lemoncurd Trail by Josie Goble

For 9-10 year old girls

Crash! And there lay Kim's father in the dirty alley, soaked to the skin and covered in mud and blood, his day's takings from the shop, gone! Then there was poor old Bridie, eighty-six years old and robbed of all her shopping!

"Why?" asks Kim. "Who would do such things?"

Horrified, she wishes she were back at Blamtree, with her dear old pal Jaimie, far away from this miserable new district where folks were mean enough to steal from frail old ladies and mug friendly, hard-working shopkeepers.

But her new chum, Colin, cheers her up. "Keep your eyes and ears open," he tells her, and by so doing they get their first clue. But was it such a mistake for folk to be seen eating lemoncurd sandwiches? What a lot Kim finds she has to write to Jaimie as she sets out with Colin – *"On the Lemoncurd Trail"*.

(124 pages) £5.00

All of these books – *The Legend Of Cairn*, *Sandy's Holiday* and *On The Lemoncurd Trail* can be purchased via our website at www.riverrunpress.co.uk.

www.ingramcontent.com/pod-product-compliance
Ingram Content Group UK Ltd.
Pitfield, Milton Keynes, MK11 3LW, UK
UKHW021331070726
13610UKWH00011B/30

9 780954 002435